THE ULTIMATE
HOW TO DRAW
CUTE ANIMAL

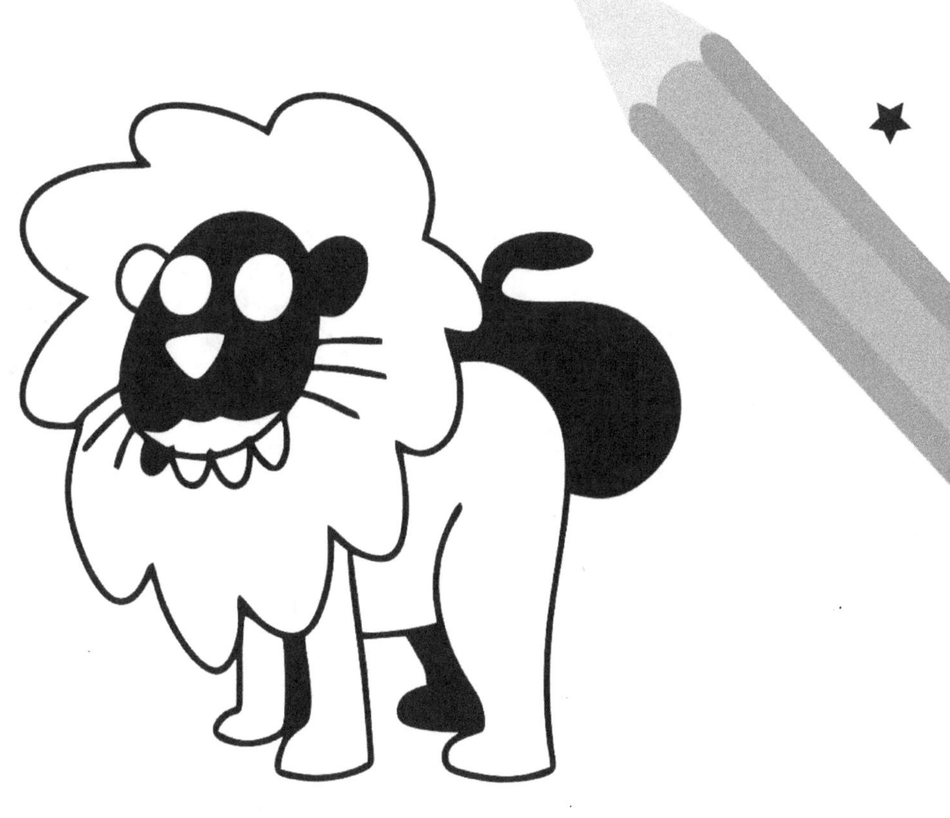

Nevaeh caddel

THIS BOOK BELONGS TO

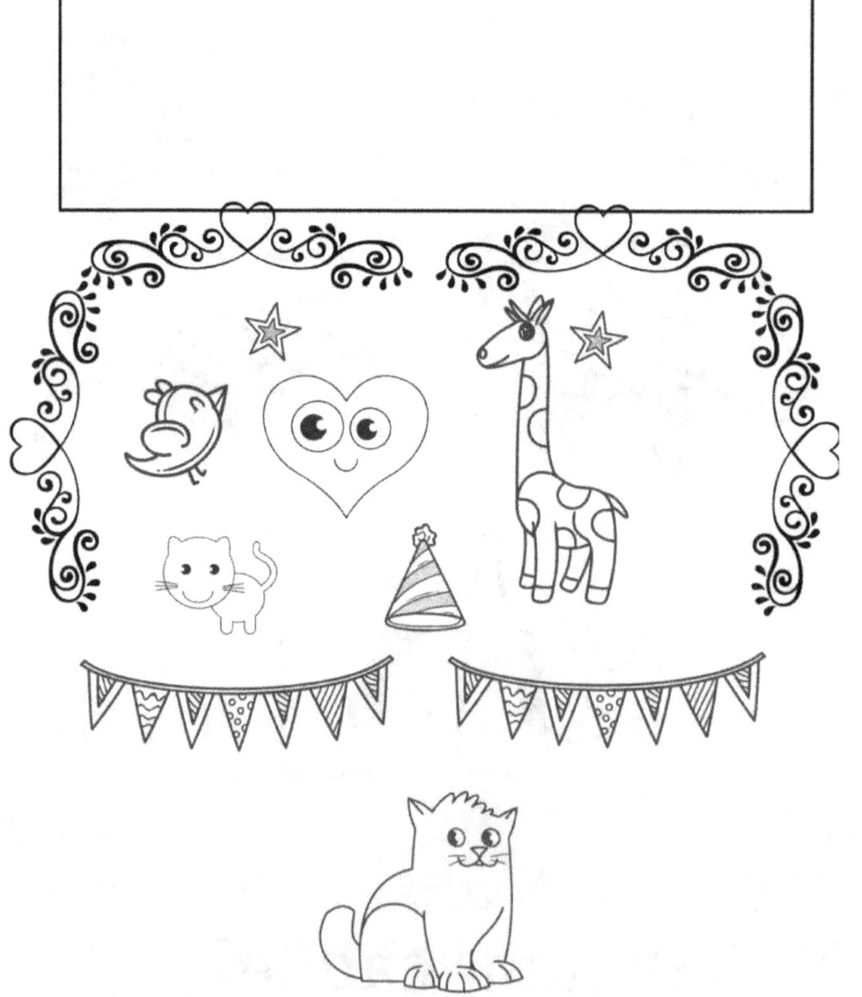

INTRODUCTION

Harry, a dedicated father and aspiring artist, set out to locate the ideal guide to teach his children how to sketch lovely animals. He came across "The Ultimate How to Draw Cute Animals for Kids" book after many searching. He ordered the book with a hopeful heart. Their cheeks lit up with delight as Harry shared the stunning drawings and step-by-step instructions with his children. They collaborated to construct a zoo full with adorable creatures. This event not only brought the family closer together, but it also helped Harry realize his dream of becoming an artist while fostering a lifetime love of art in his children.

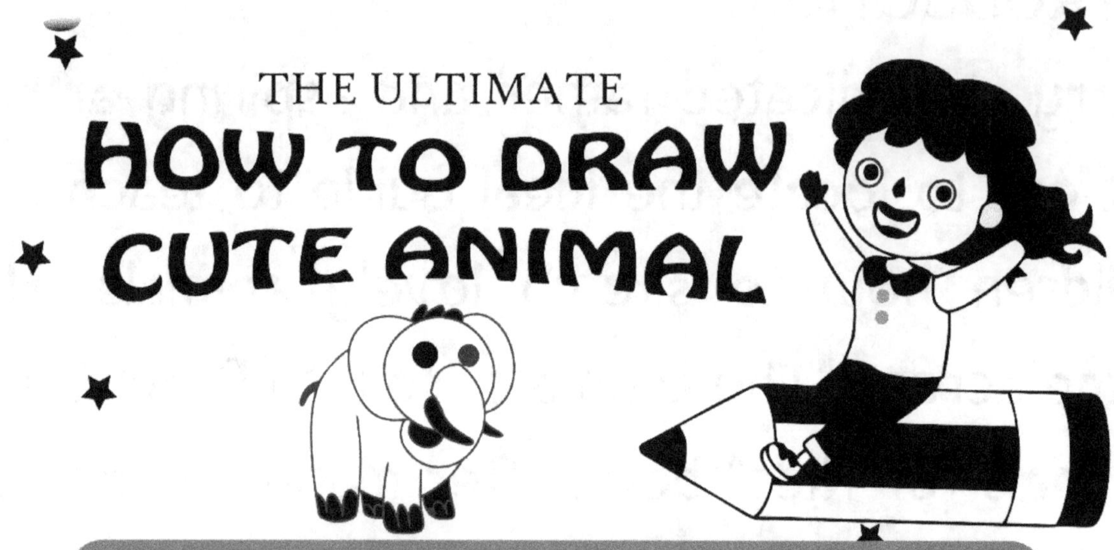

Starting to draw can be a fun and creative activity for kids. Here's a step-by-step guide for a drawing book designed for children:

STEP 1: GATHER SUPPLIES Begin by collecting essential drawing materials, such as blank sheets of paper, pencils, erasers, and a set of colored pencils or crayons. Ensure the workspace is well-lit and comfortable.

STEP 2: BASIC SHAPES Teach kids to start with basic shapes like circles, squares, triangles, and rectangles. These can serve as building blocks for more complex drawings.

STEP 3: LINES AND DOODLES Introduce the concept of different lines – straight, curved, zigzag, and dashed. Encourage kids to practice making various lines and doodles to improve their hand-eye coordination.

STEP 4: SIMPLE OBJECTS Guide them in drawing simple objects like apples, stars, and hearts using the basic shapes and lines they've learned. Keep these early drawings straightforward to build confidence.

STEP 5: ANIMALS AND CHARACTERS Move on to drawing easy animals or characters like cats, dogs, and smiley faces. Use basic shapes and lines as a foundation, and add details like eyes, mouths, and tails.

STEP 6: COLORING Explain the concept of coloring within the lines, using various shades to make drawings more vibrant. Encourage creativity in choosing colors.

STEP 7: PRACTICE Emphasize the importance of practice. Kids should continue drawing regularly to improve their skills. Provide blank pages for them to express their ideas freely.

The wonderful thing about art is that you may use whatever tool you desire! Yes, that's correct! Because you are the artist, feel free to get creative with this book, but keep it simple. It's simple to learn if you use blank sheets of paper or grind paper.

Remind them that drawing takes time and practice, and it's okay to make mistakes. Positive Encouragement:

Praise their efforts and creations to boost their confidence and motivation. Explore Tutorials:

Trace The Clockwise Direction Here.

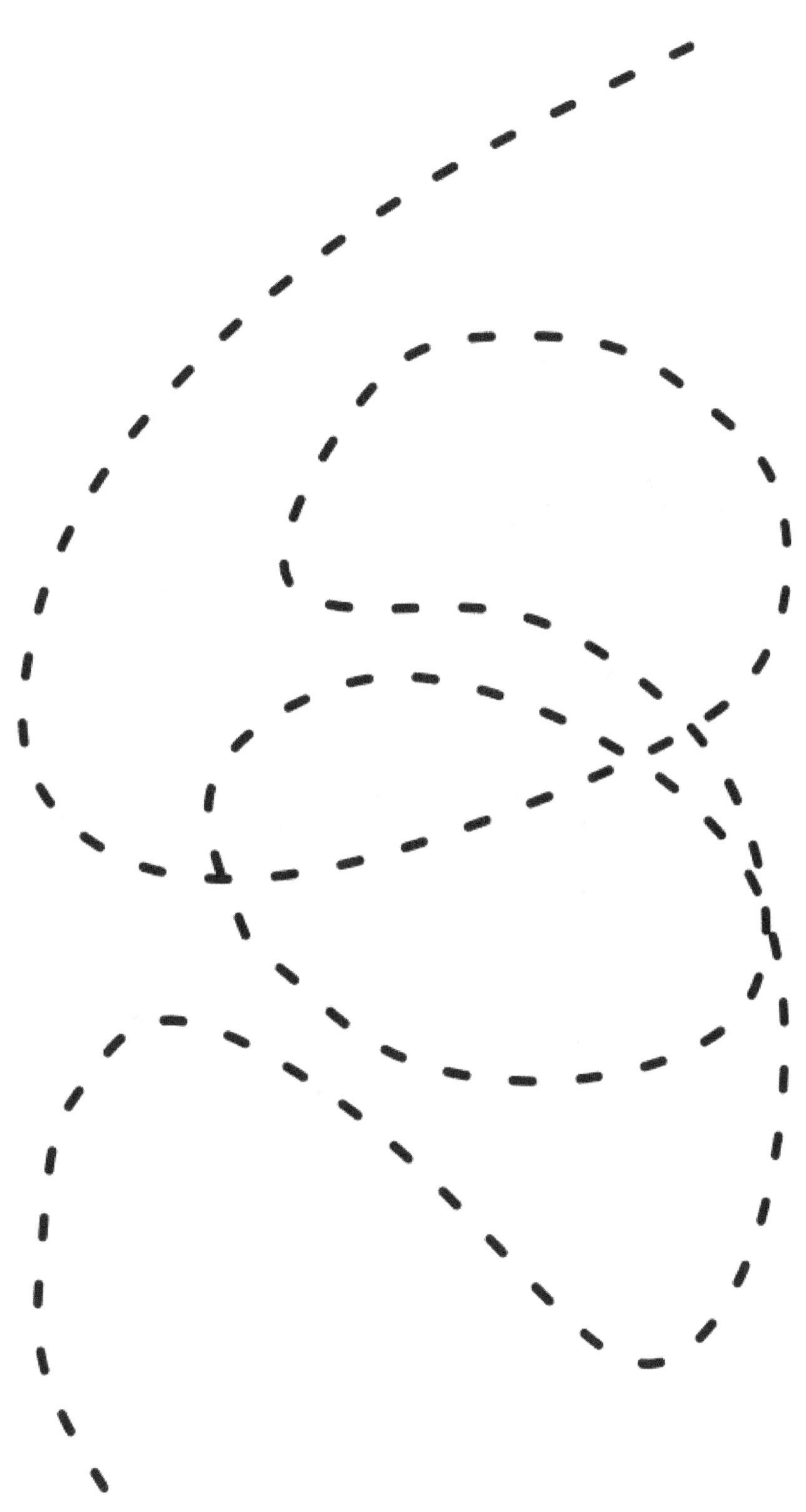

Trace the clockwise patterns below.

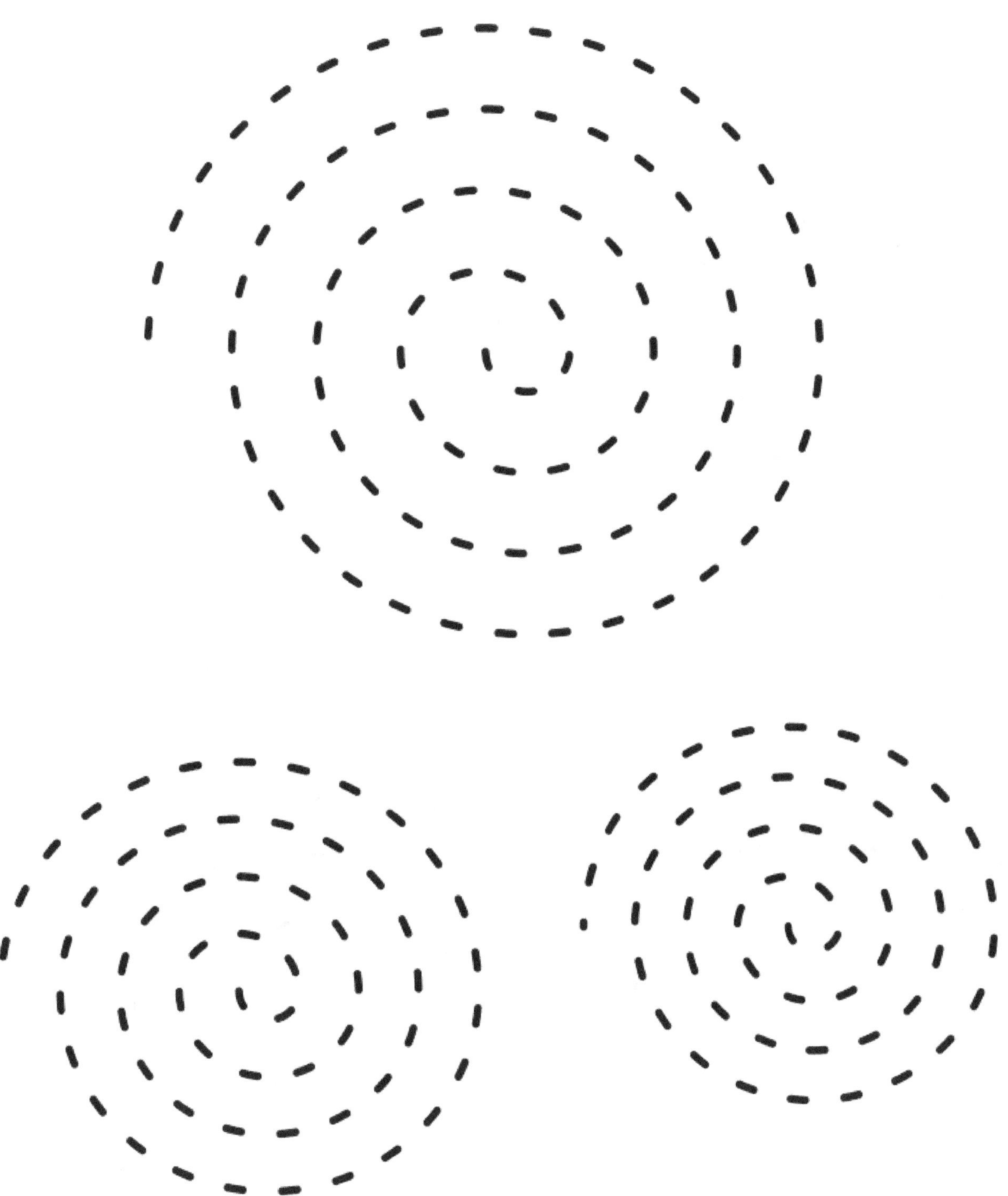

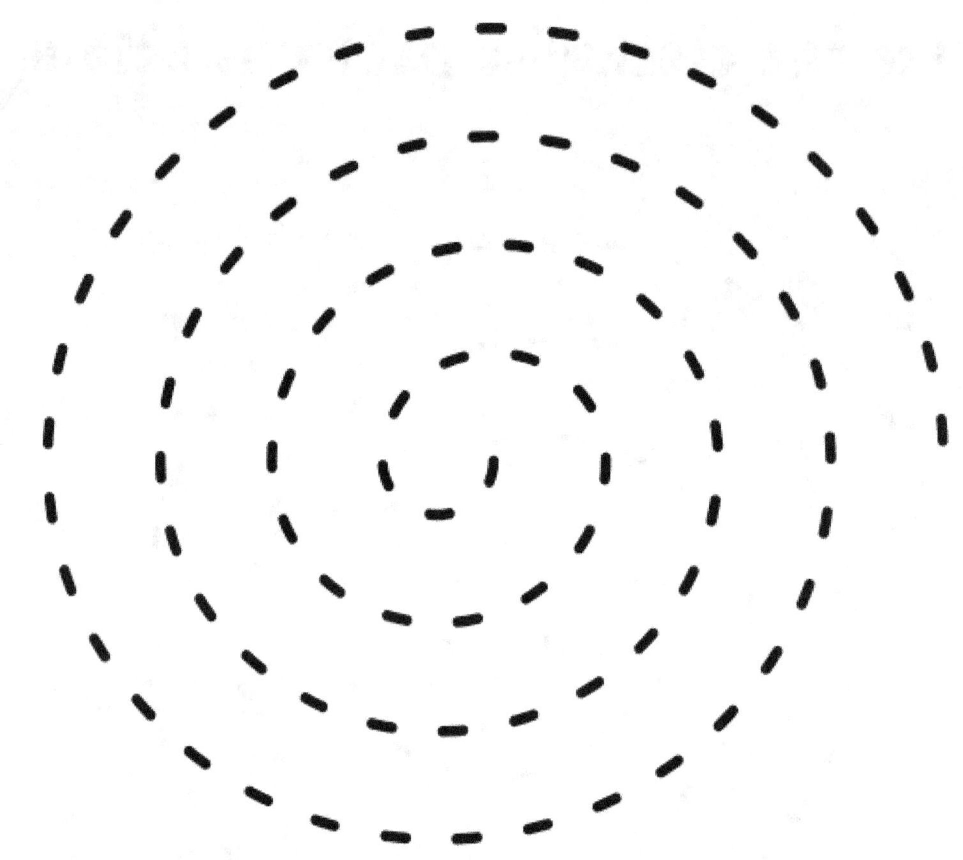

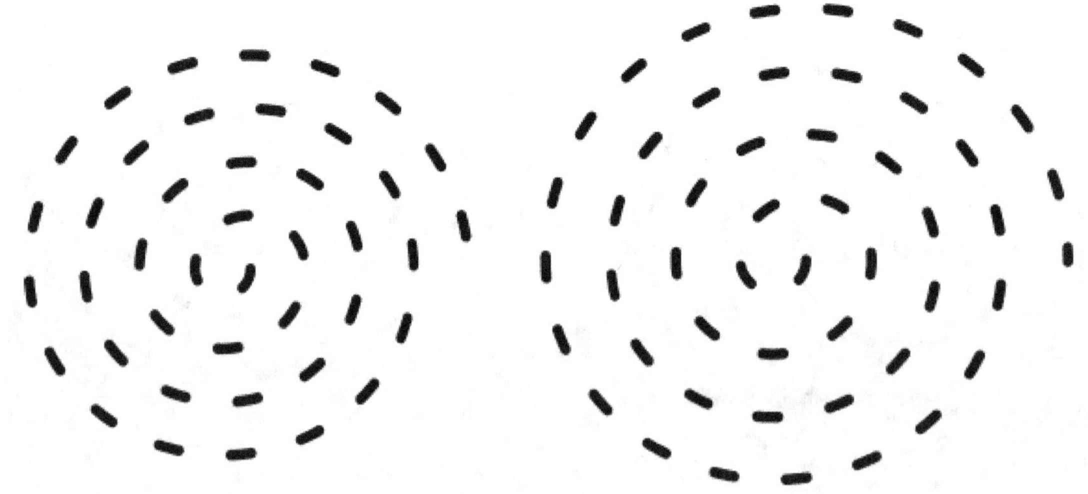

Trace the zigzag lines.

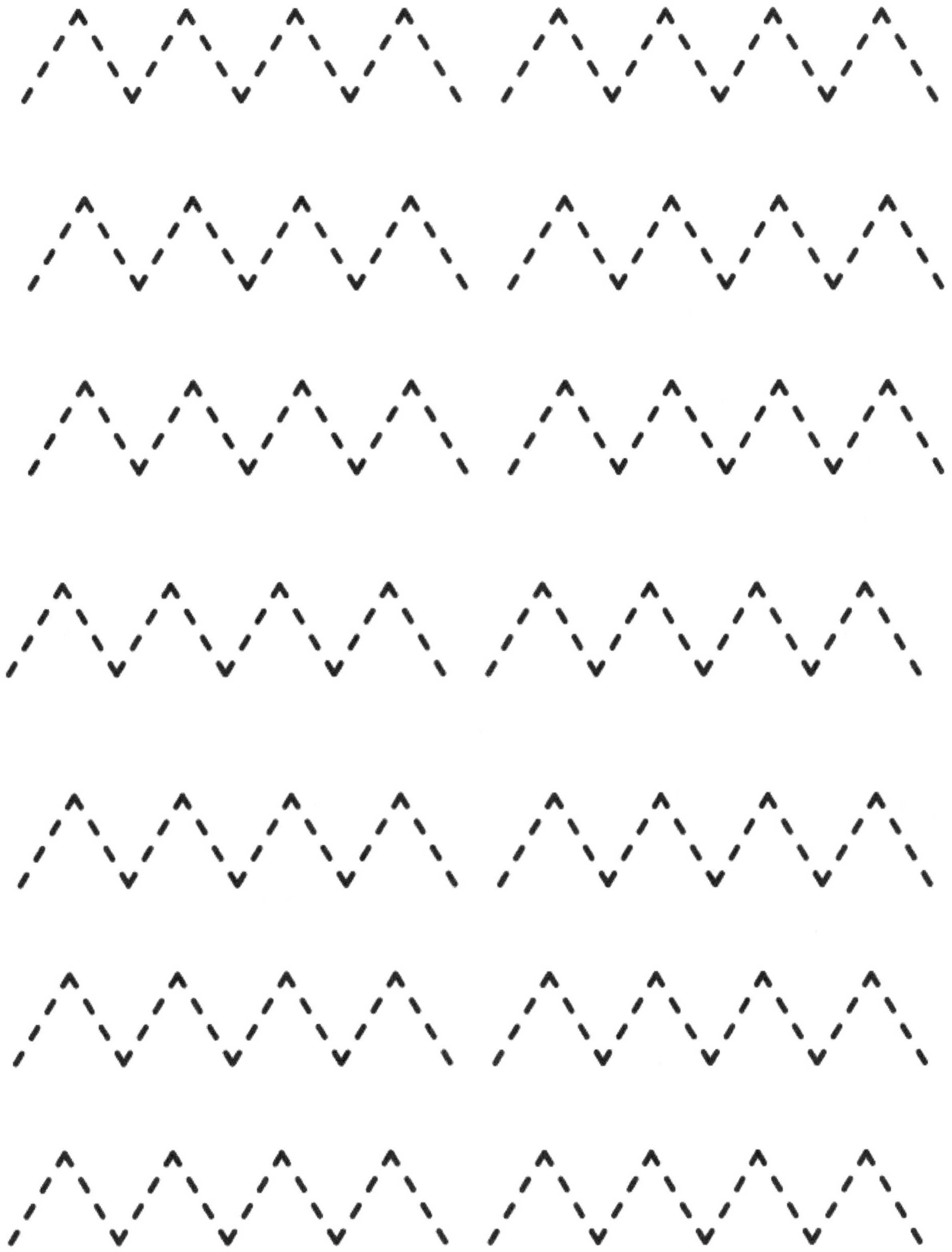

Trace the zigzag lines.

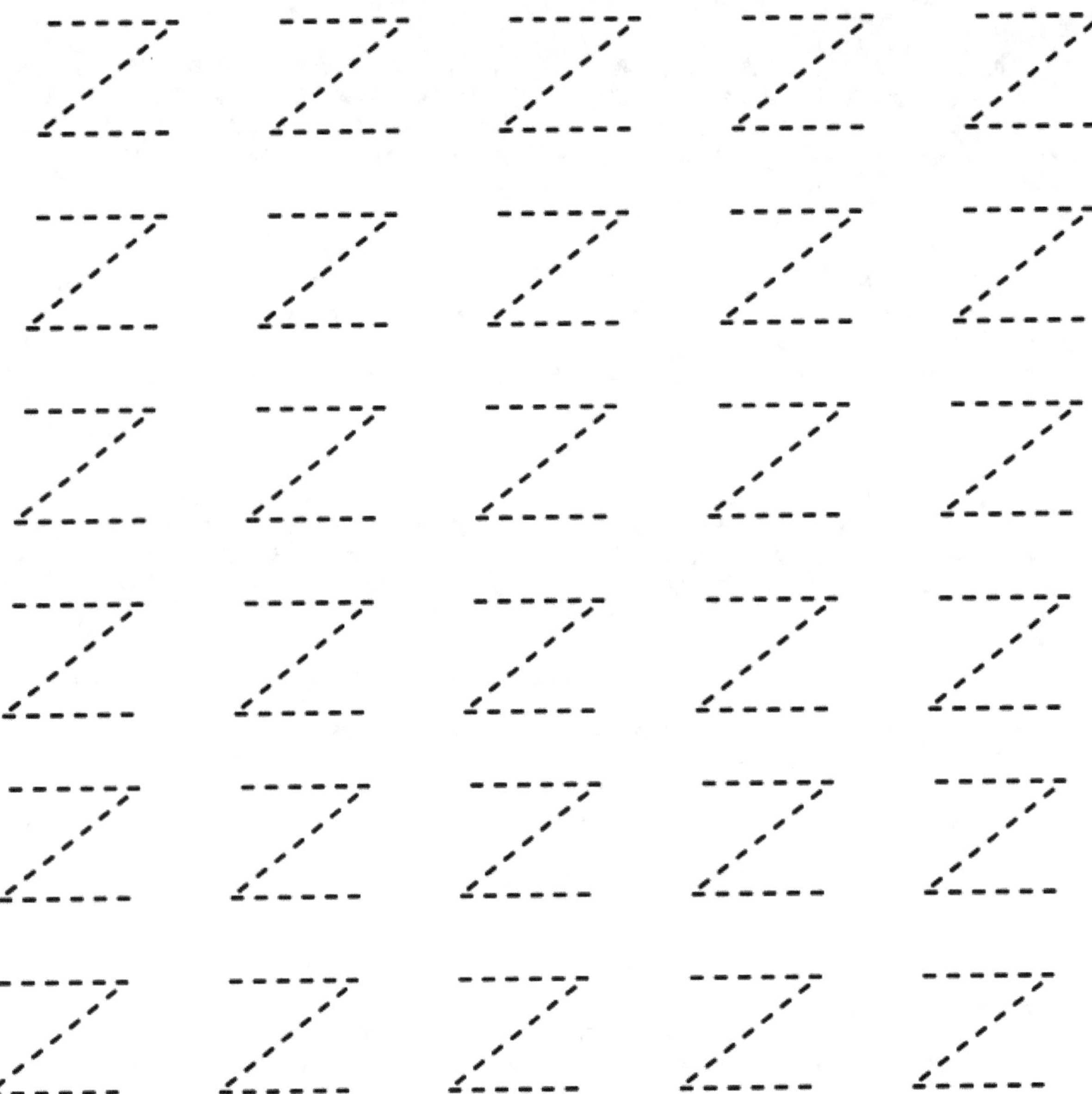

say and trace the left curves.

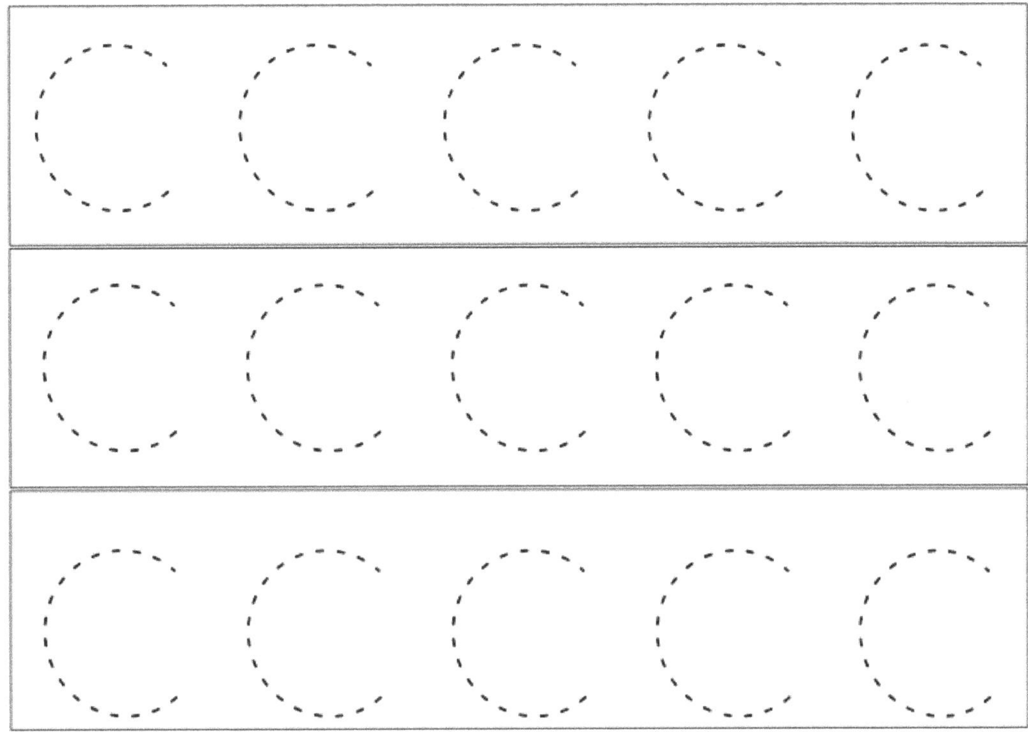

Copy the left curves.

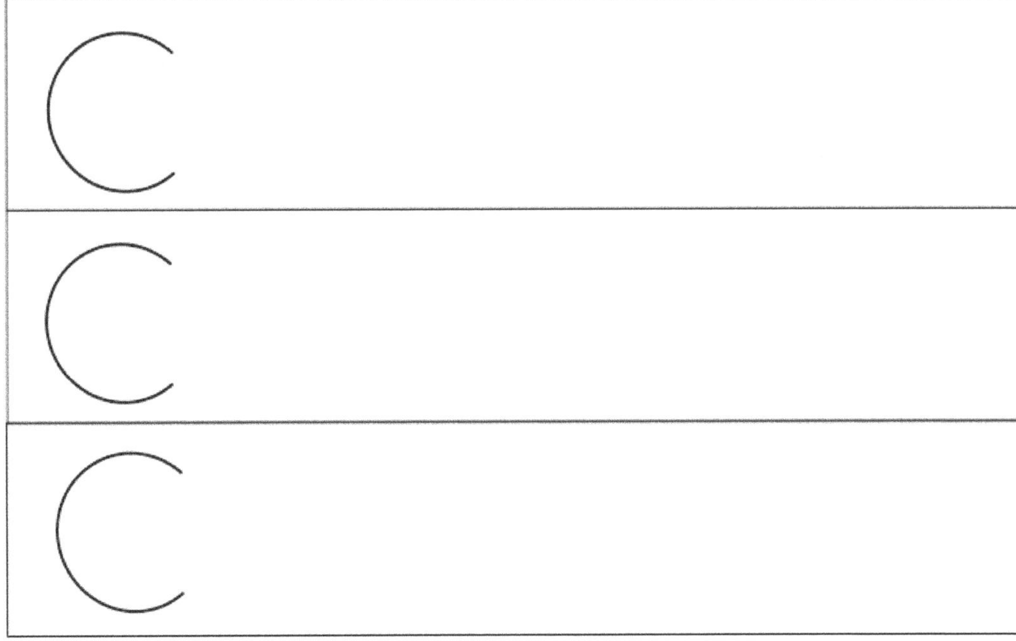

Trace the overlaping curves.

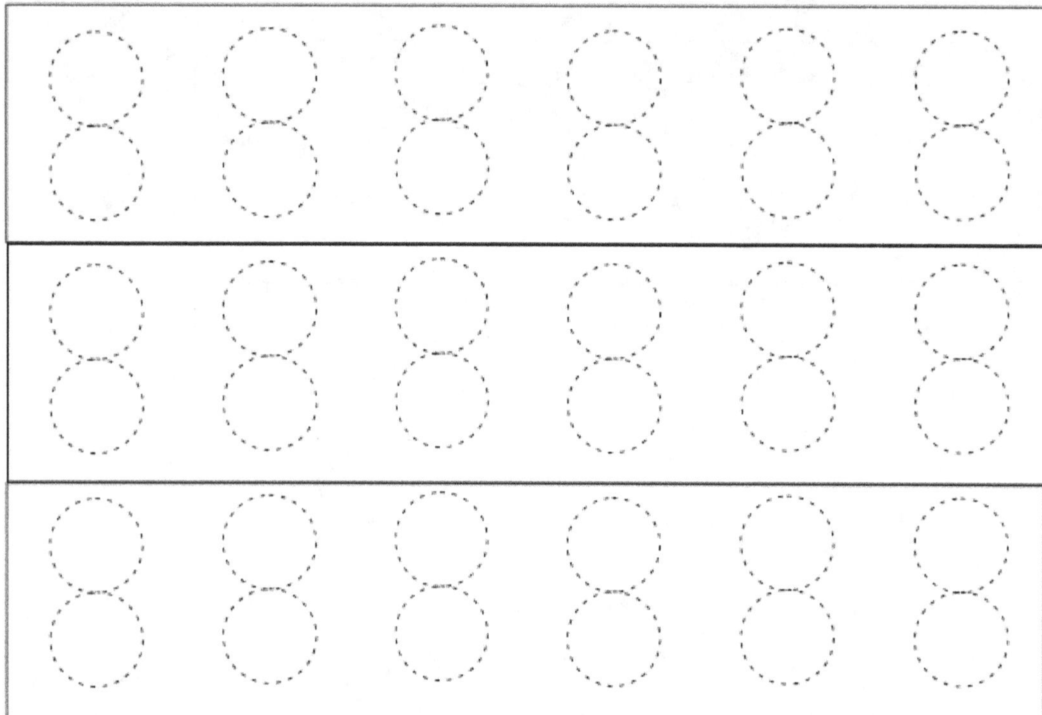

Copy the overlaping curves.

Trace each circle and draw your own in the space provided

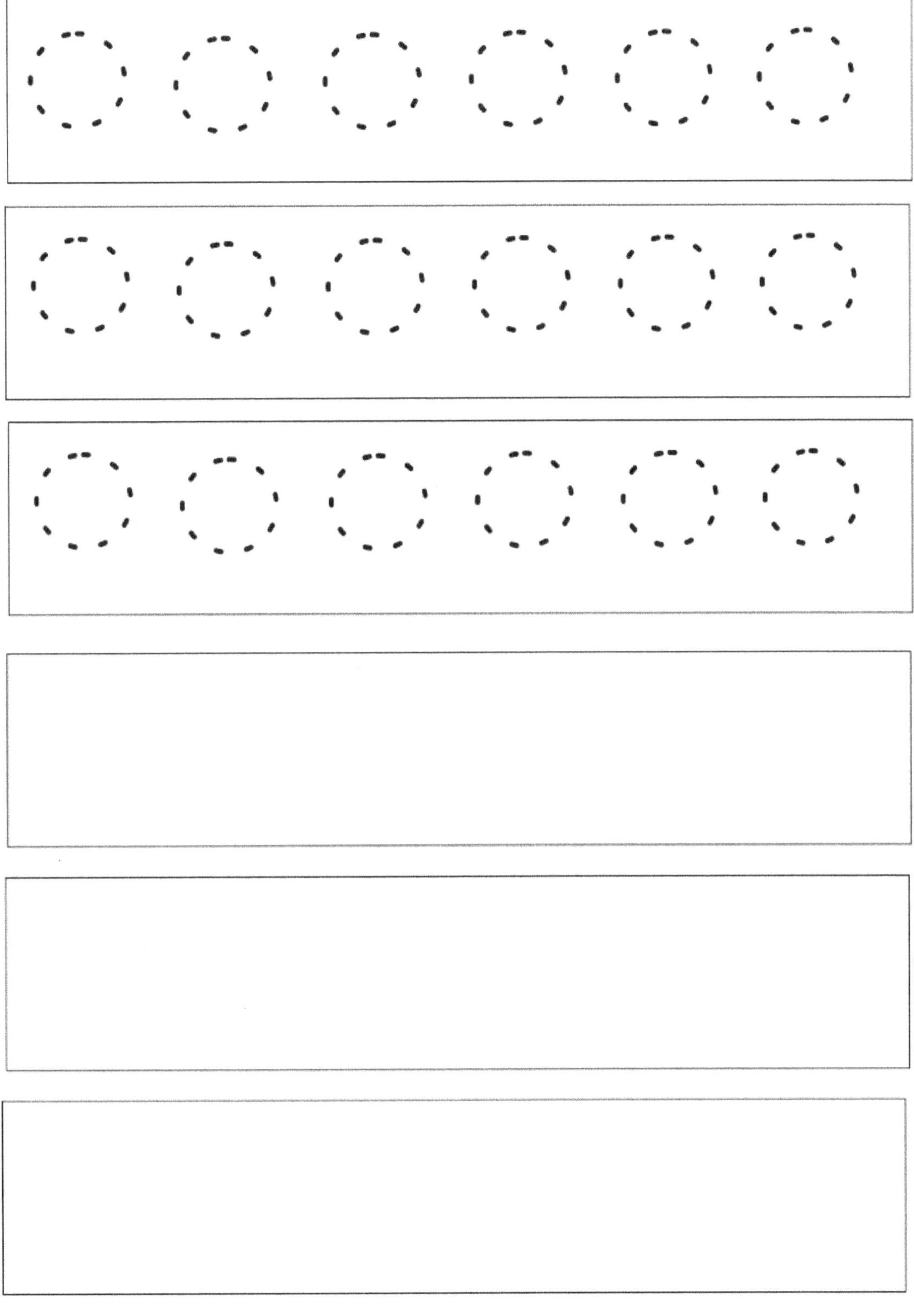

Trace The Right Curves.

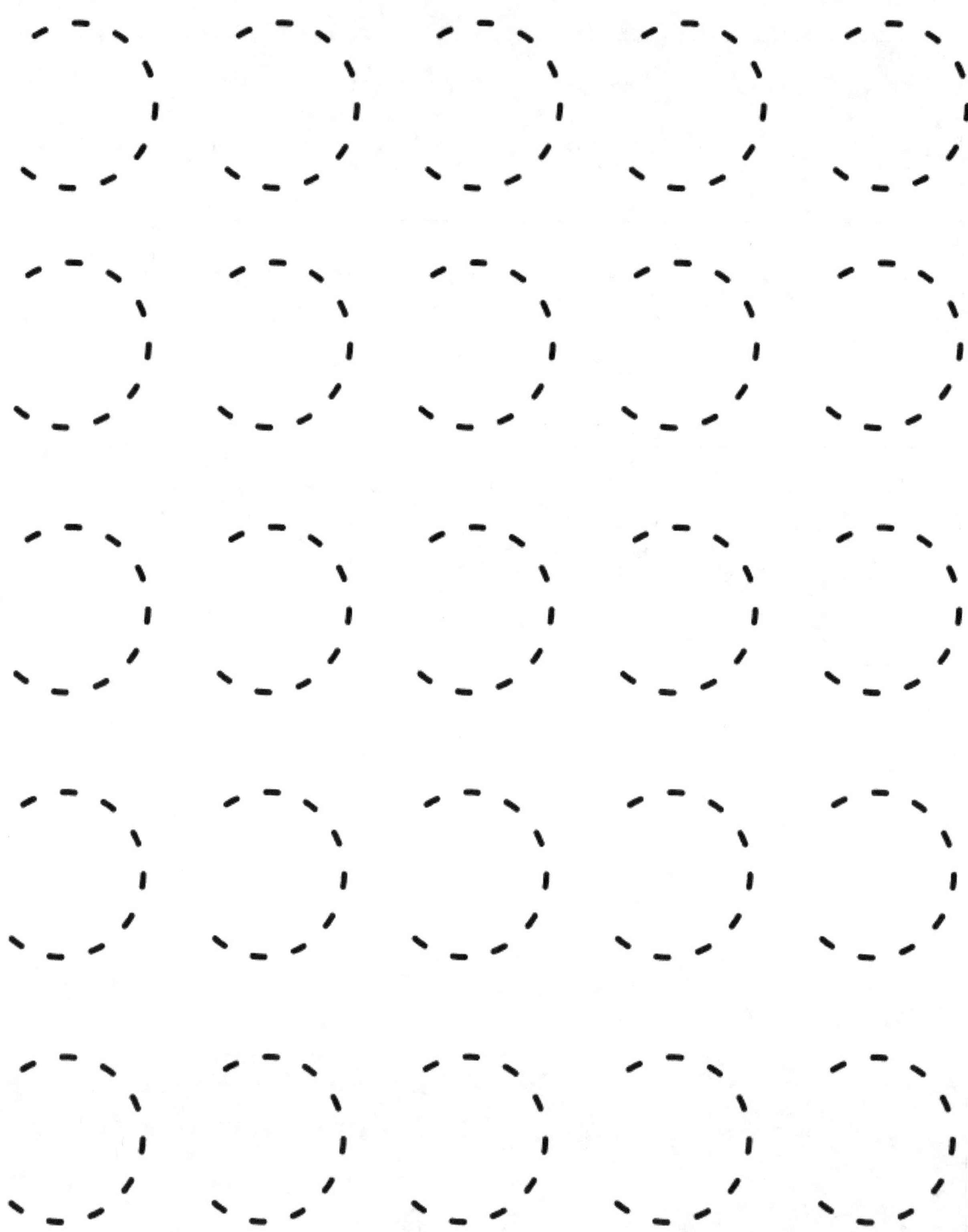

Trace and make the pattern below.

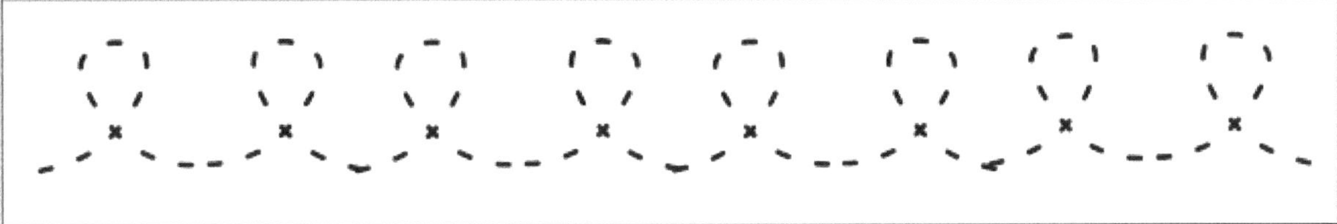

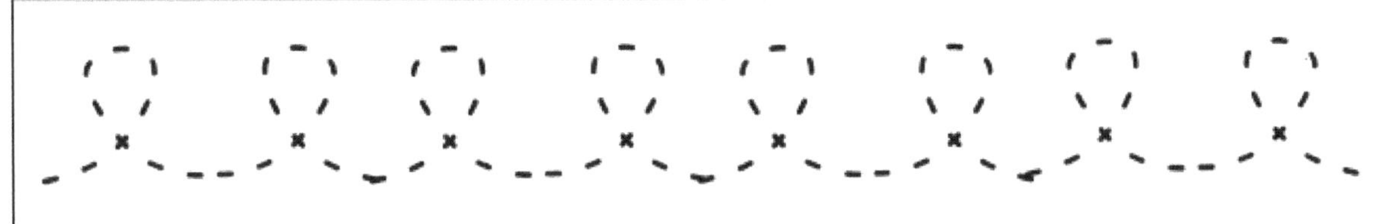

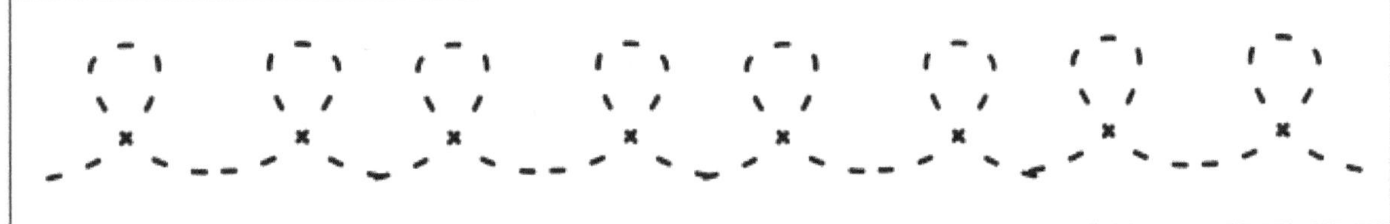

copy the pattern below.

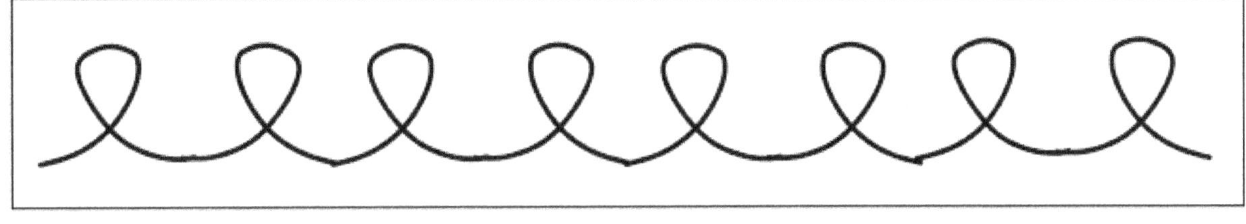

Trace the wavy lines.

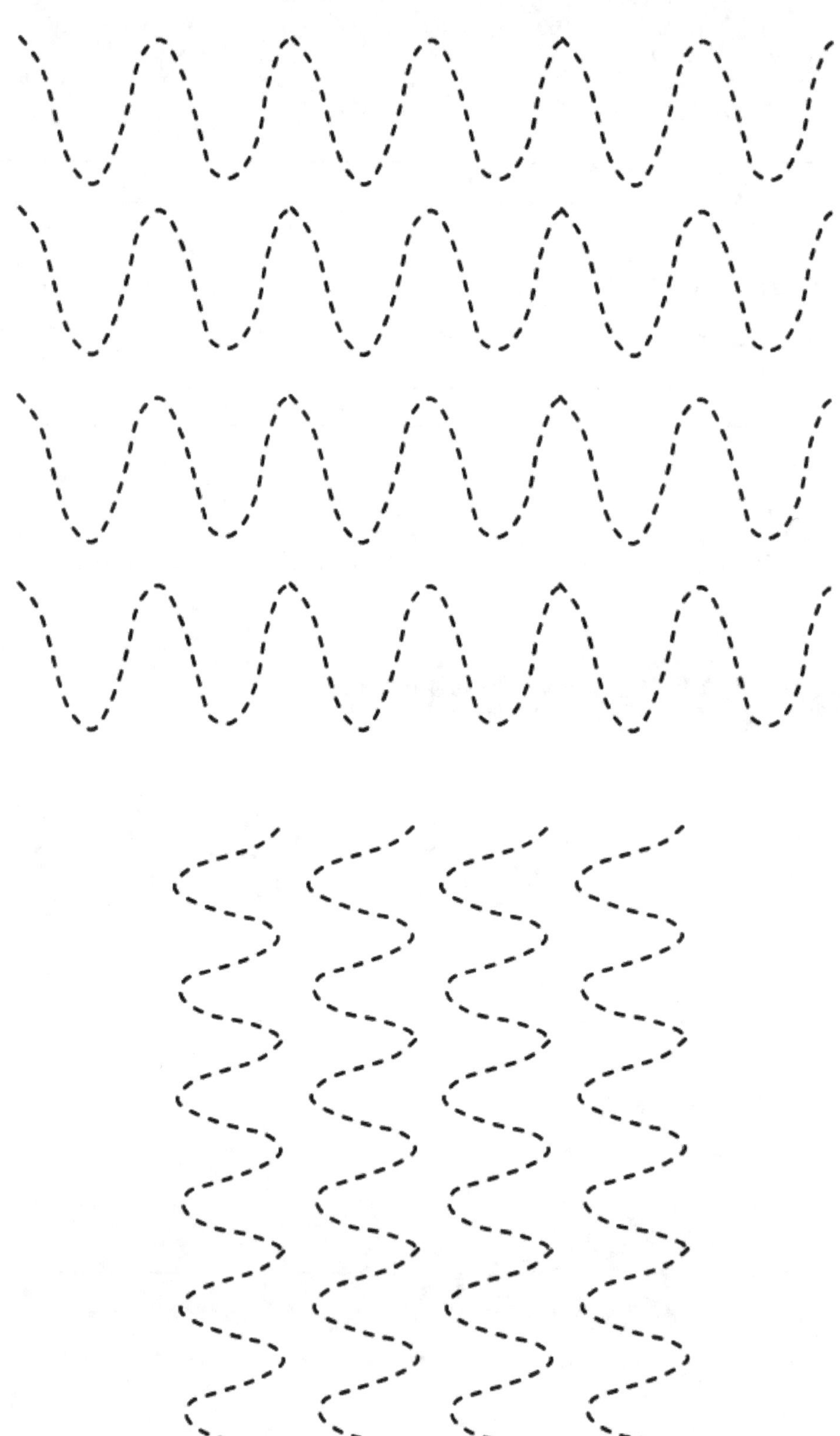

CAT

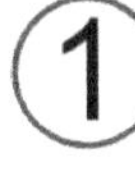
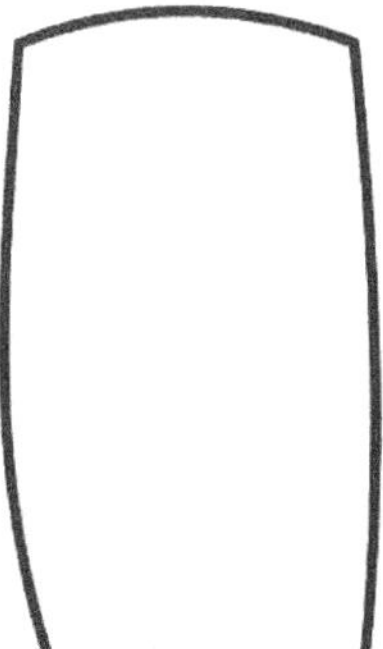

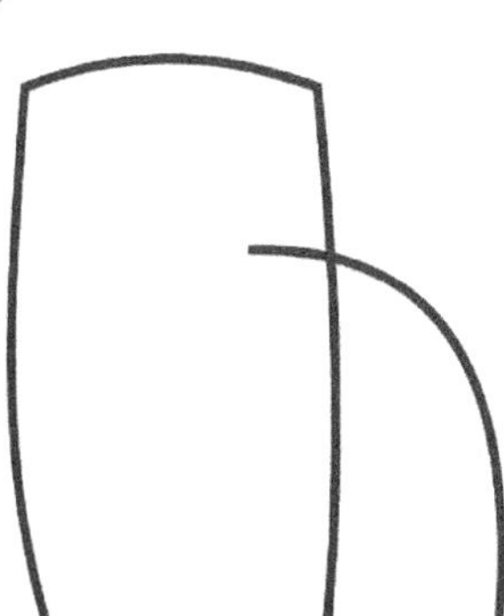
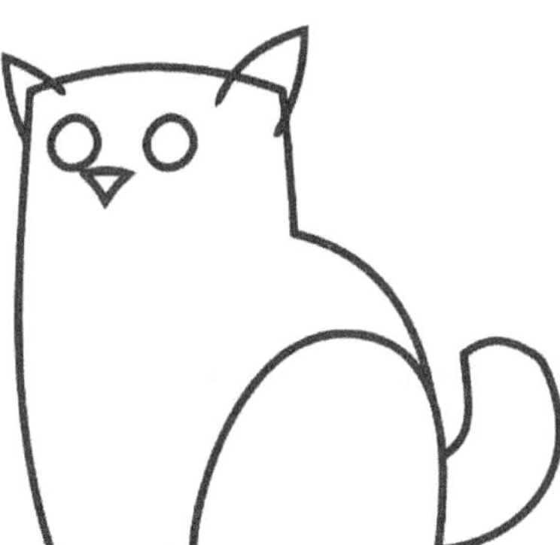

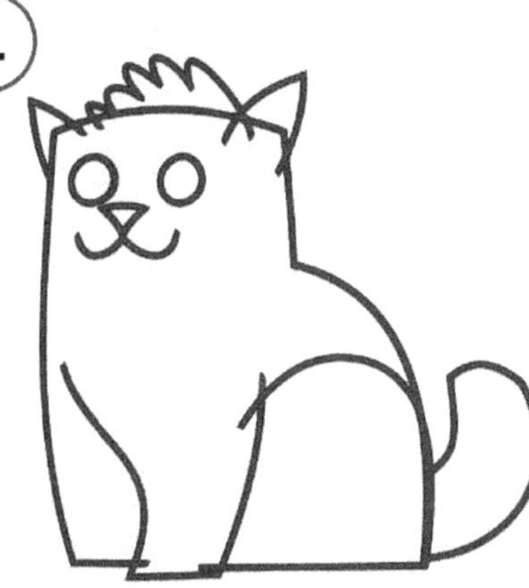
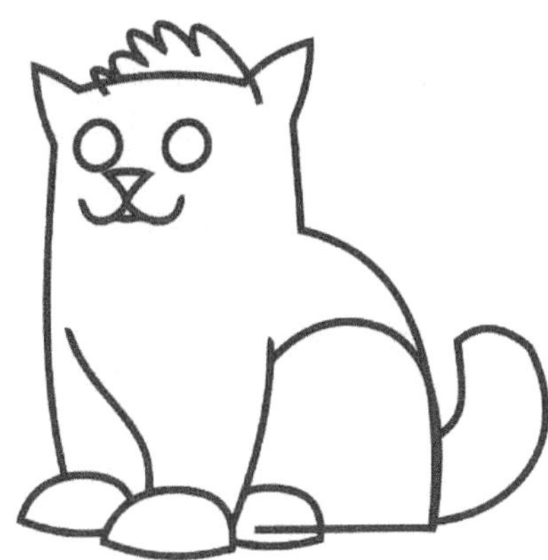
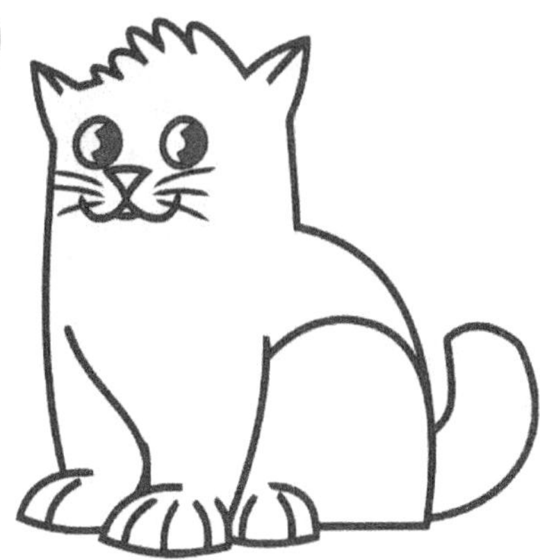

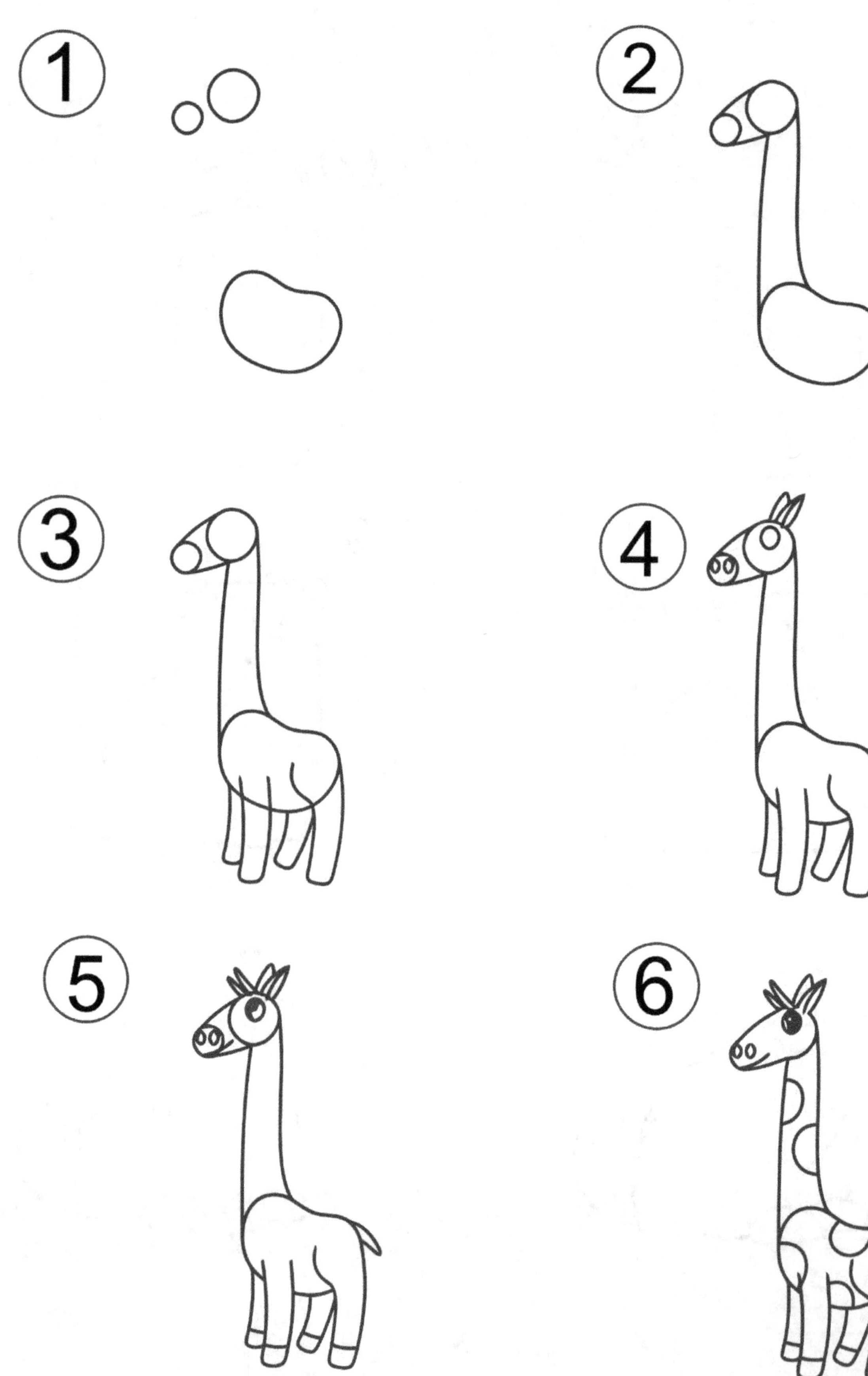

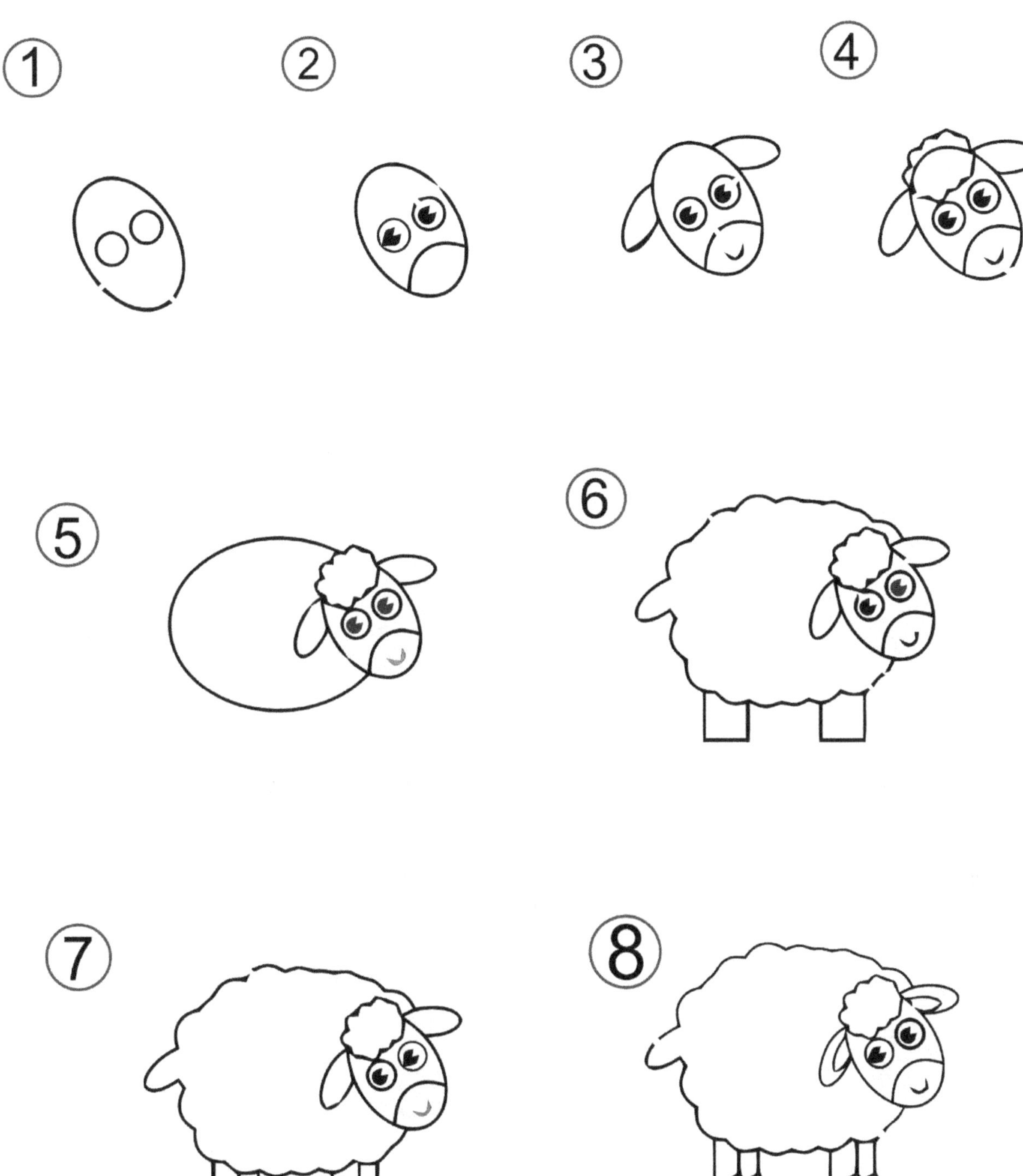

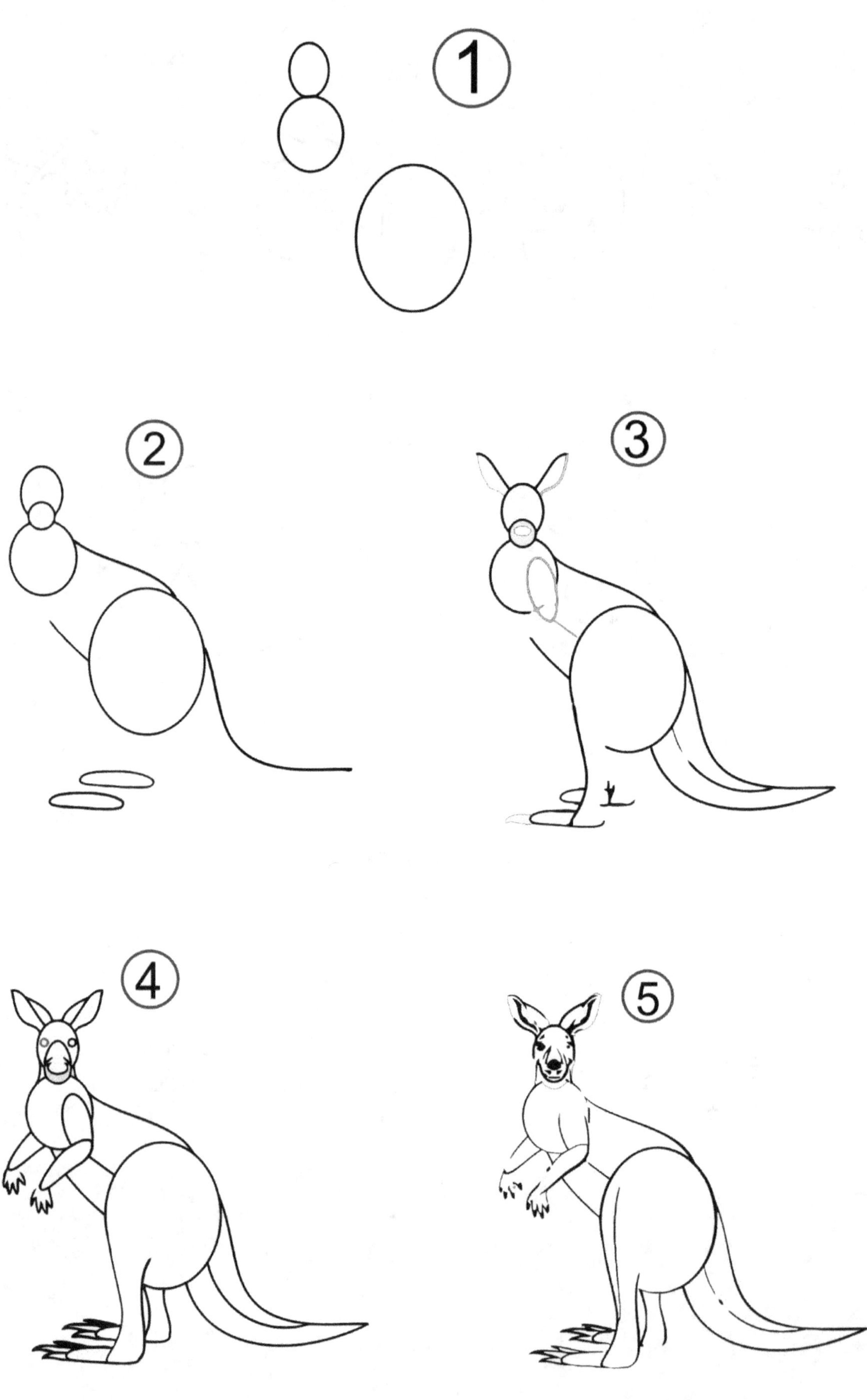

1
2
3
4
5

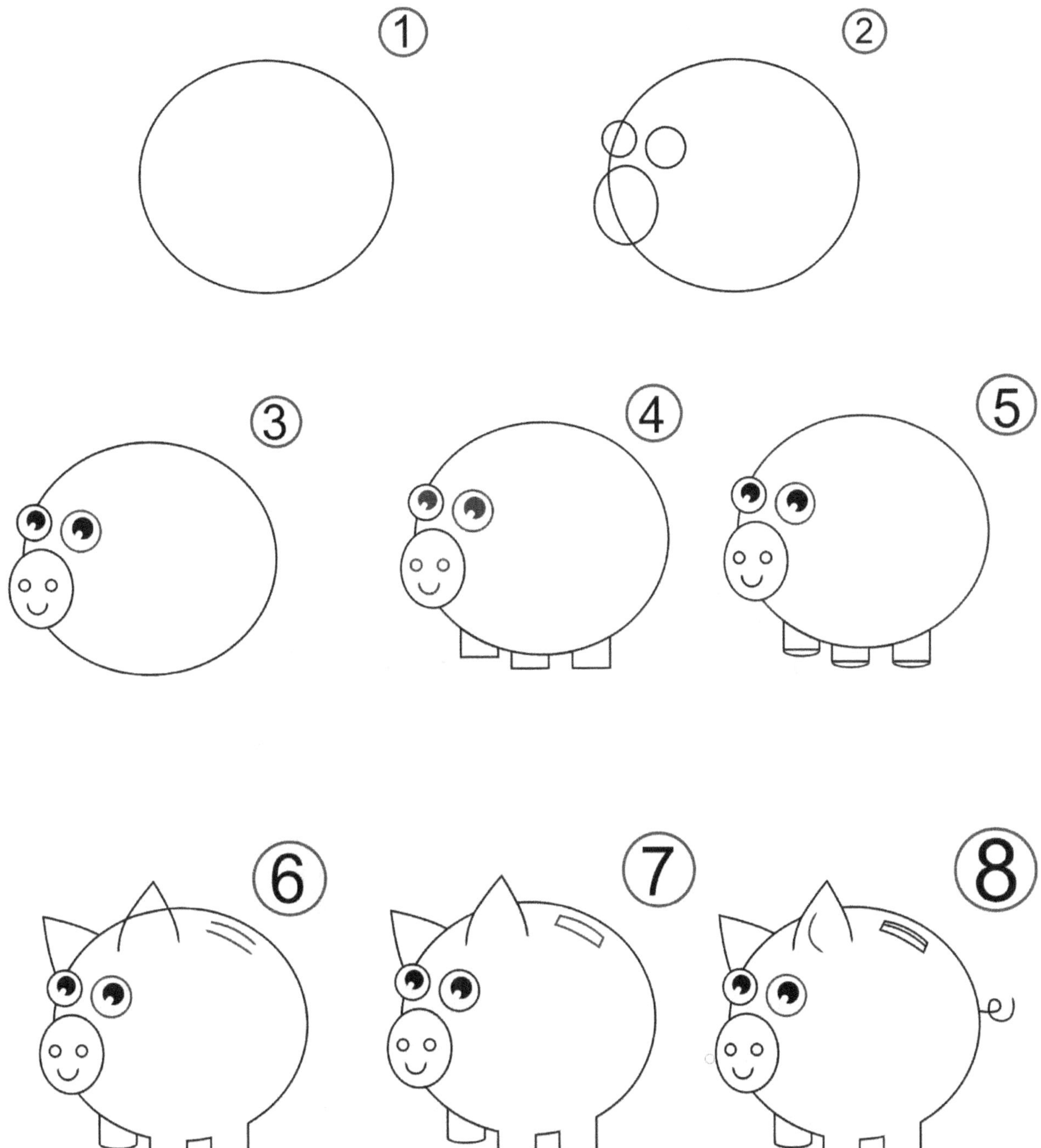

BIRD

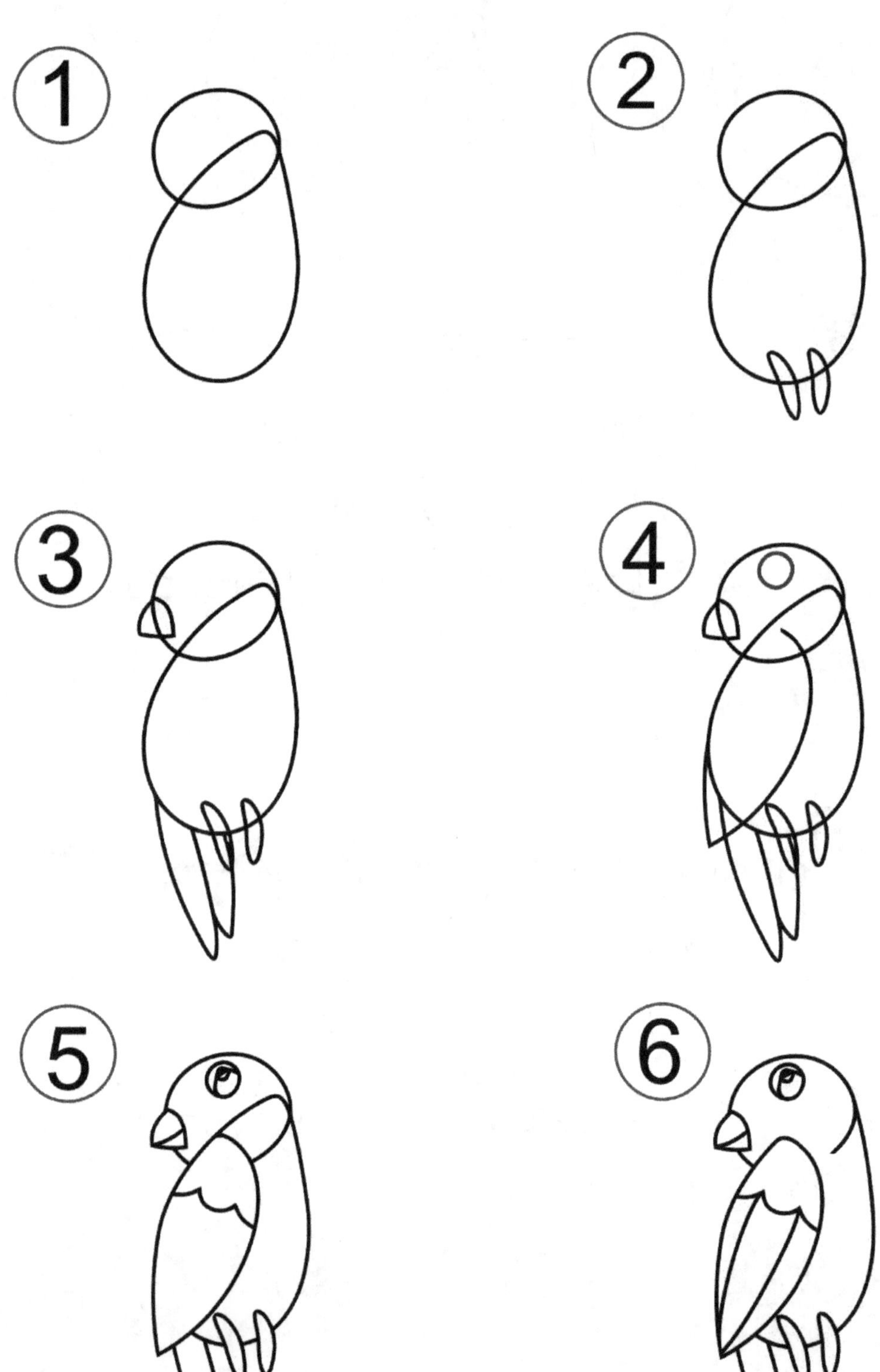

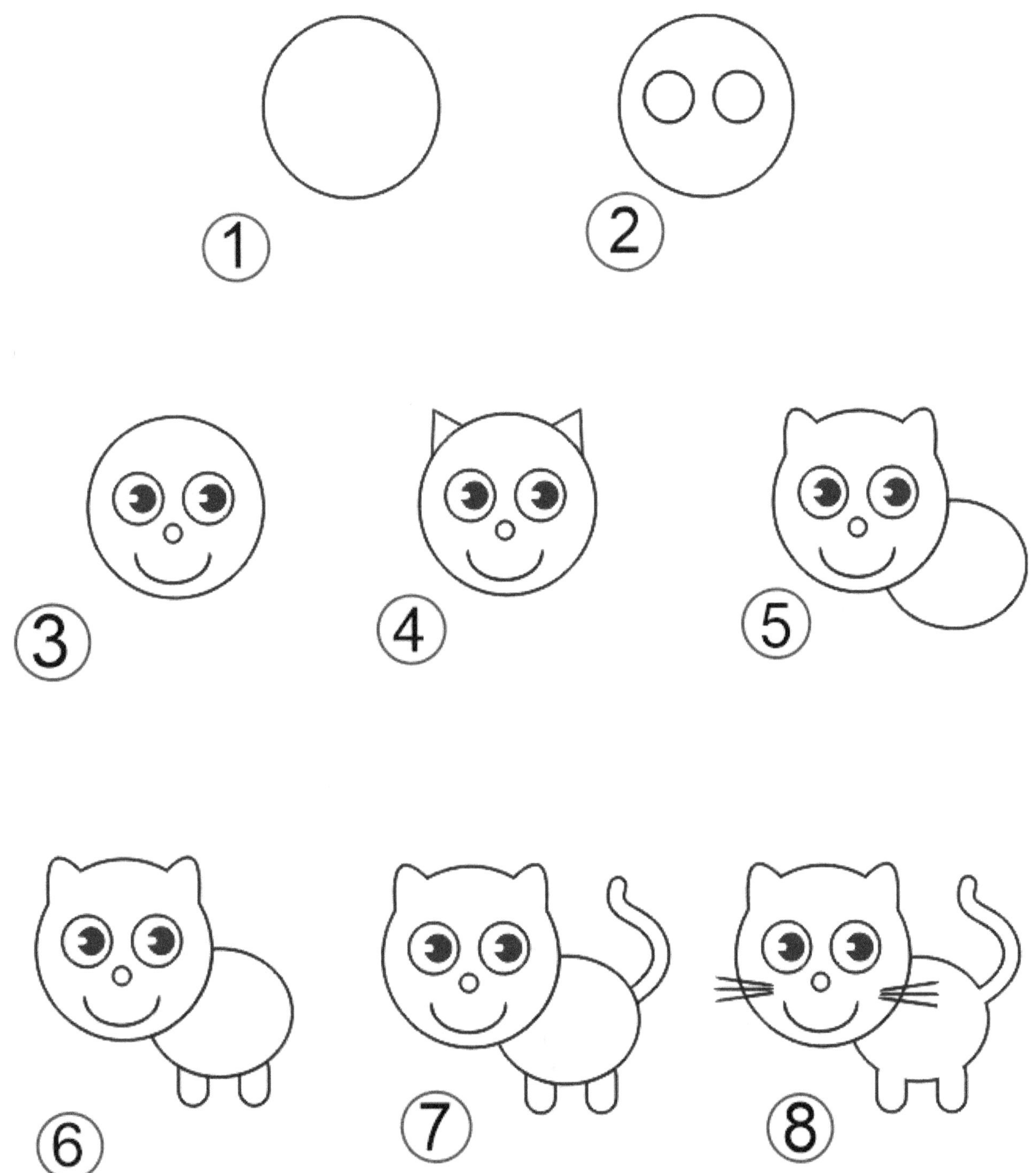

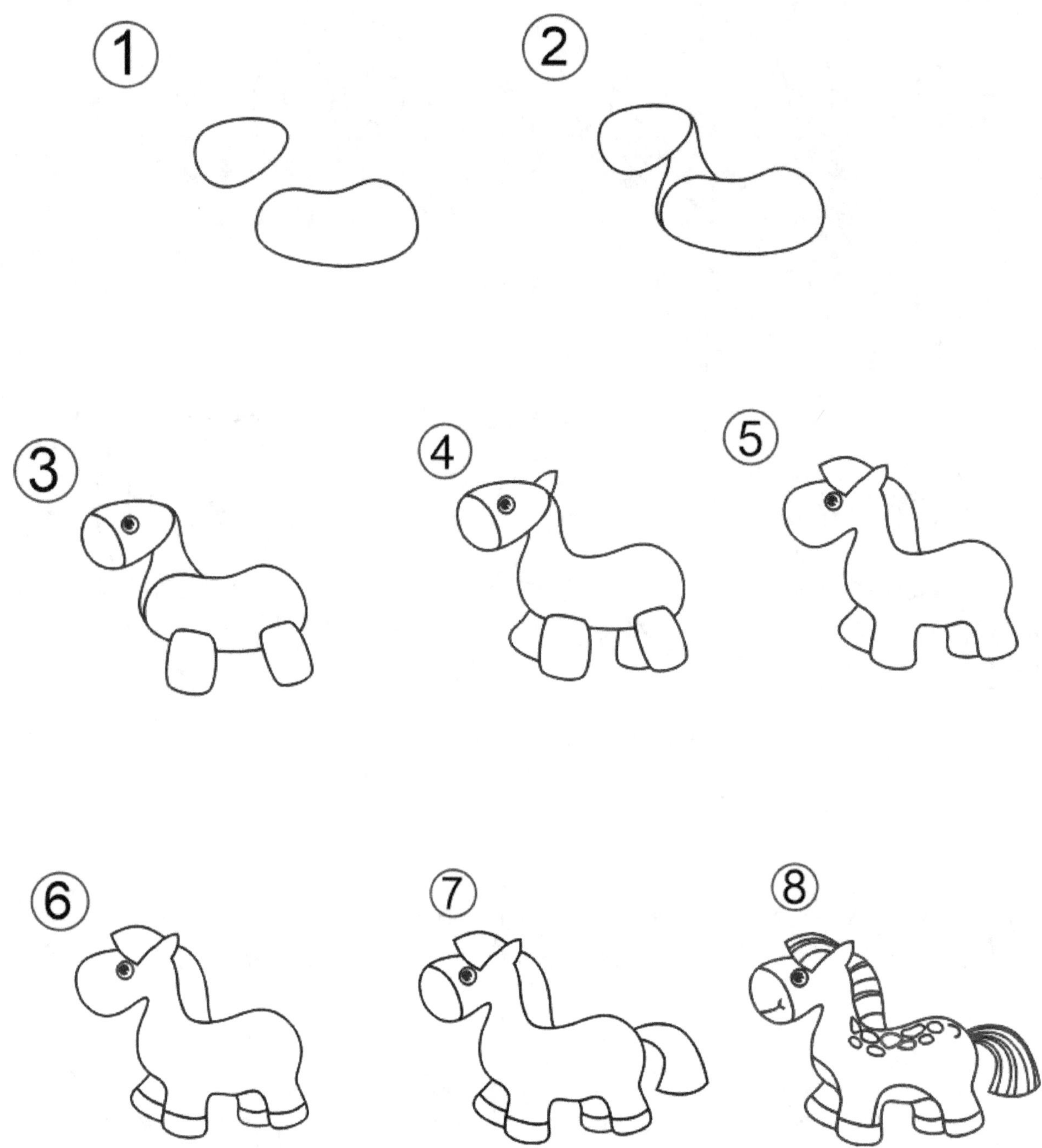

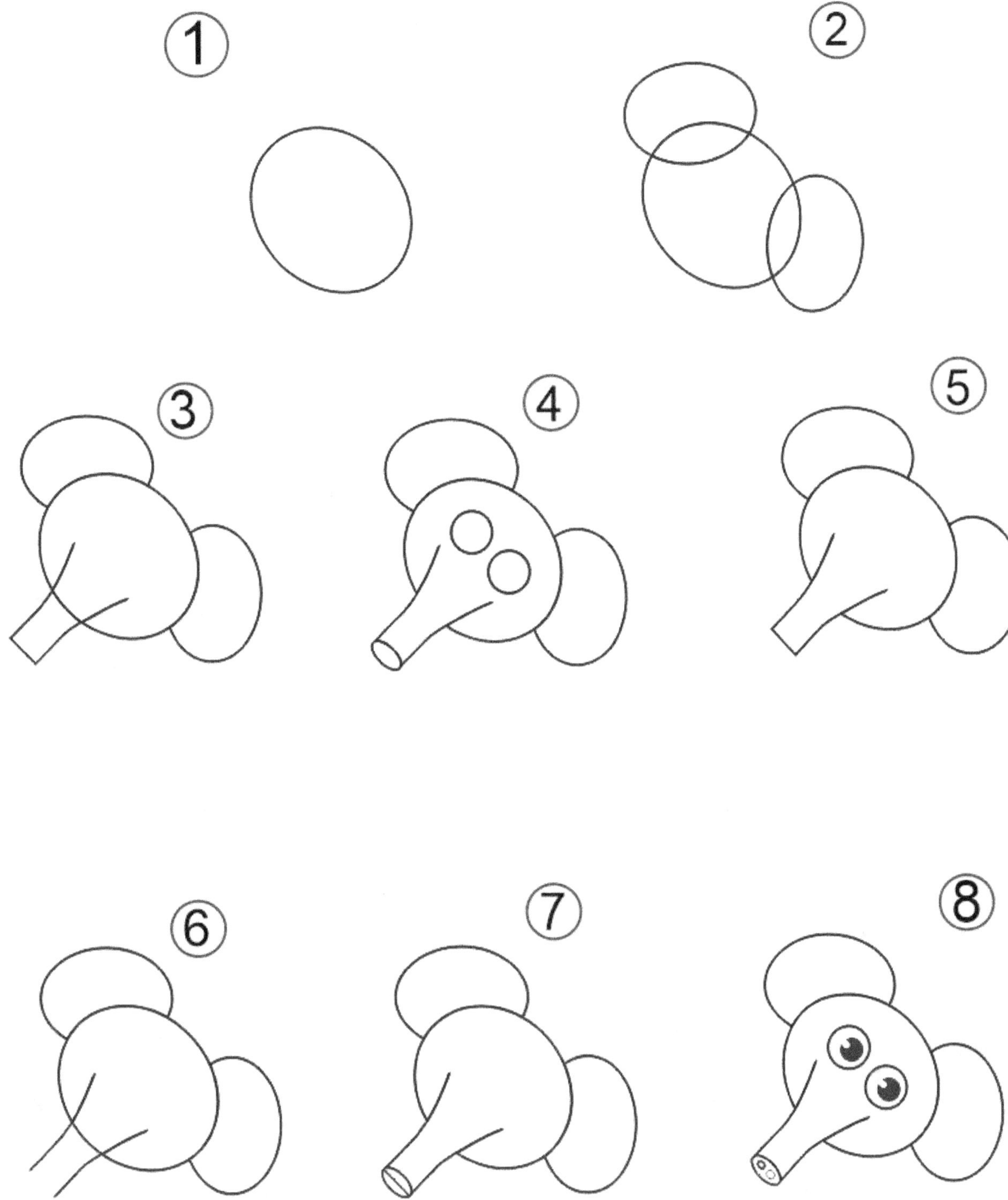

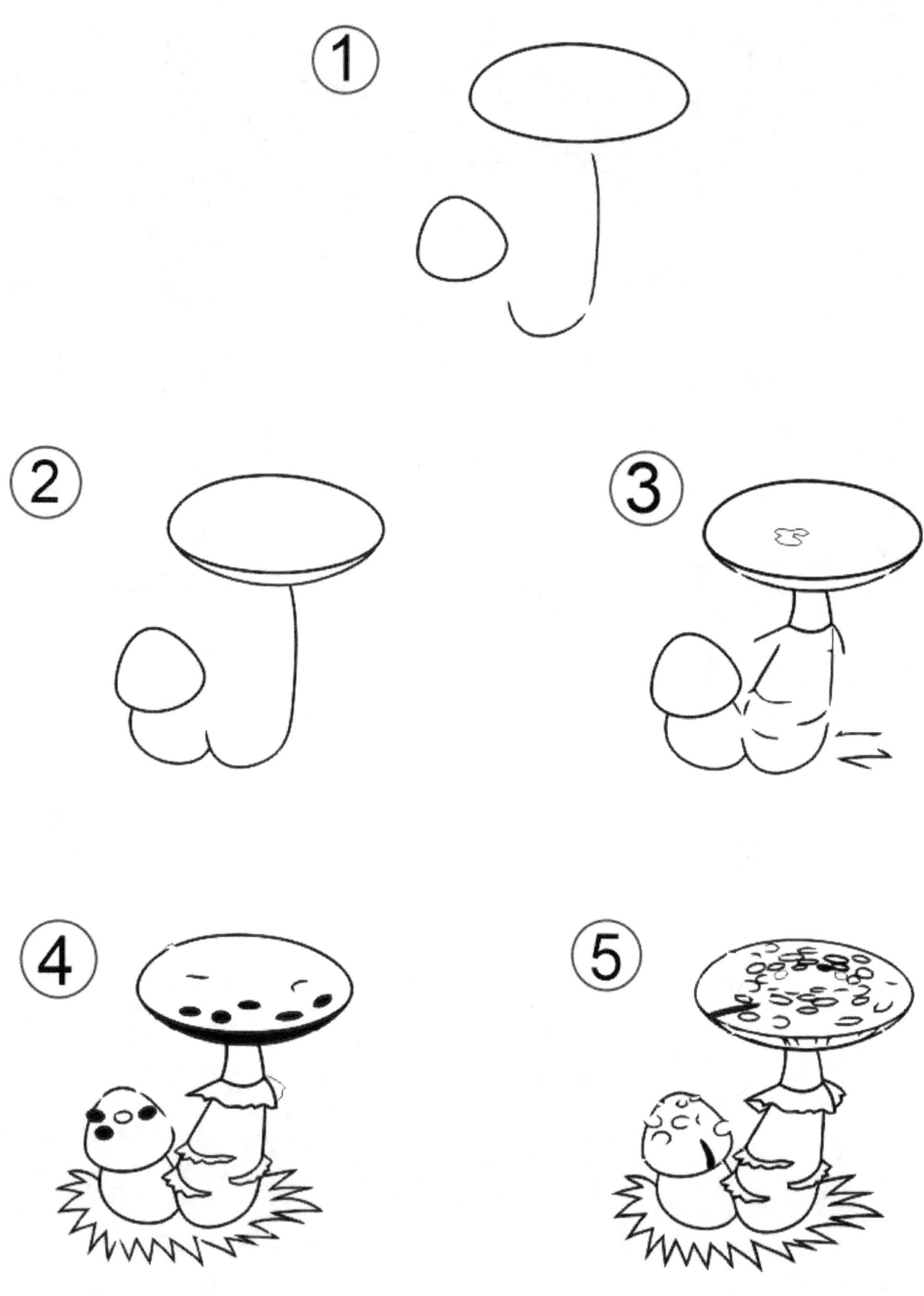

1
2
3
4
5

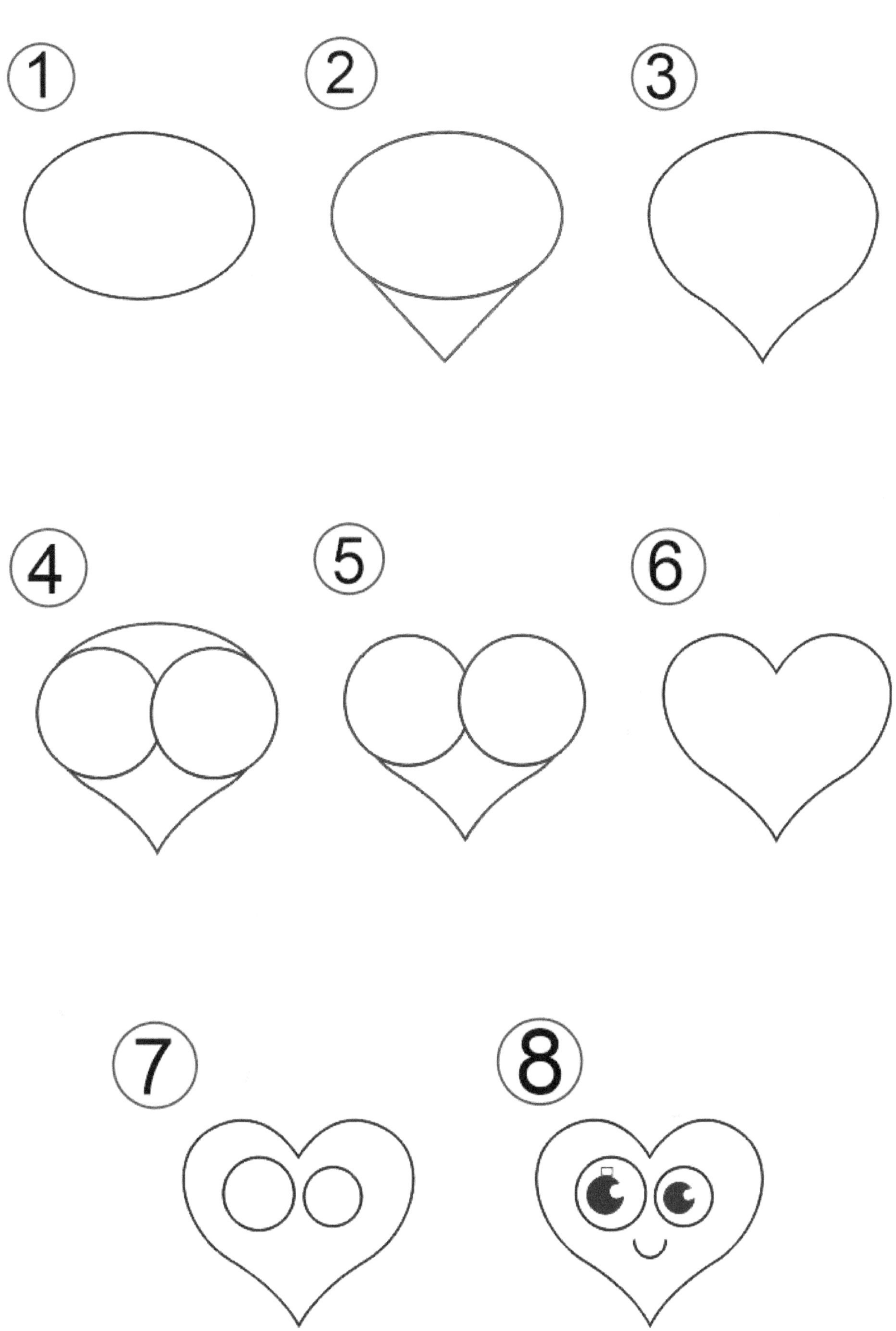

HEN

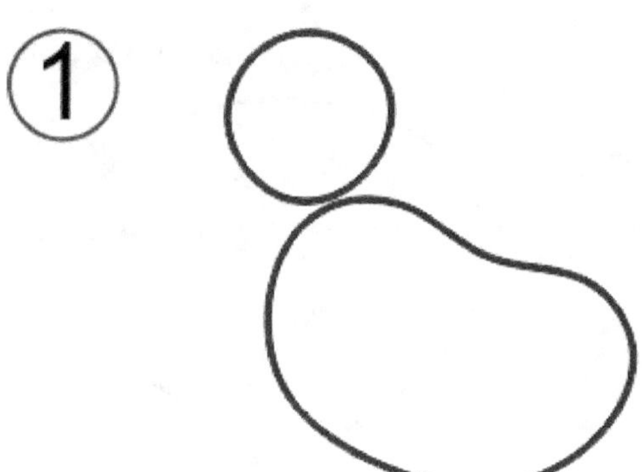

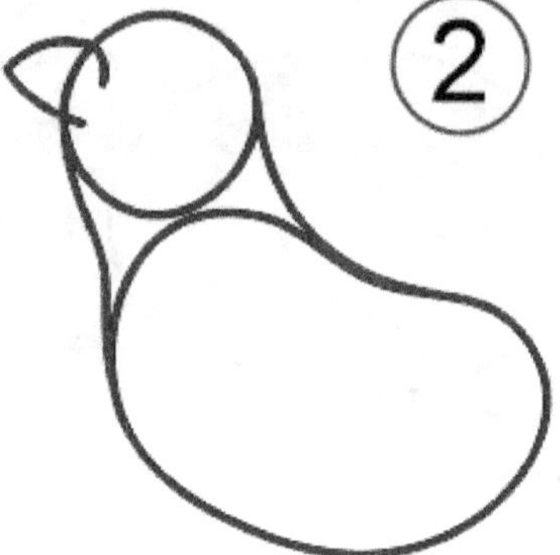

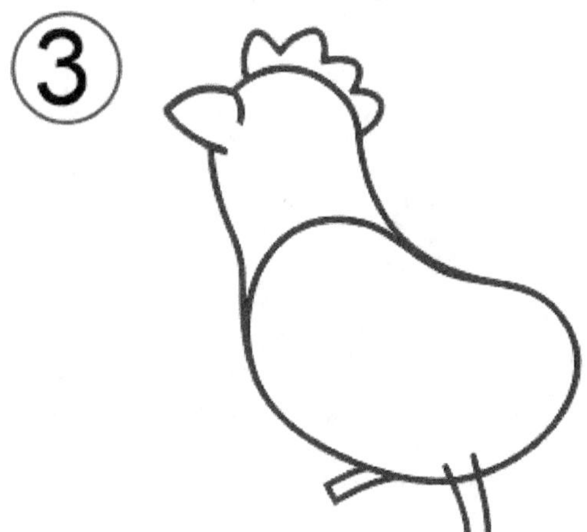

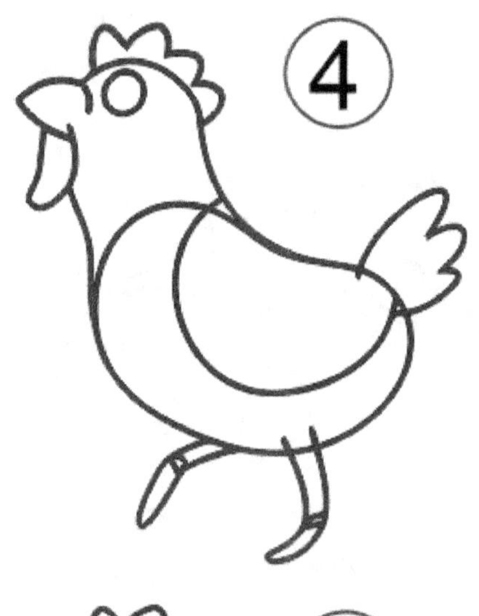

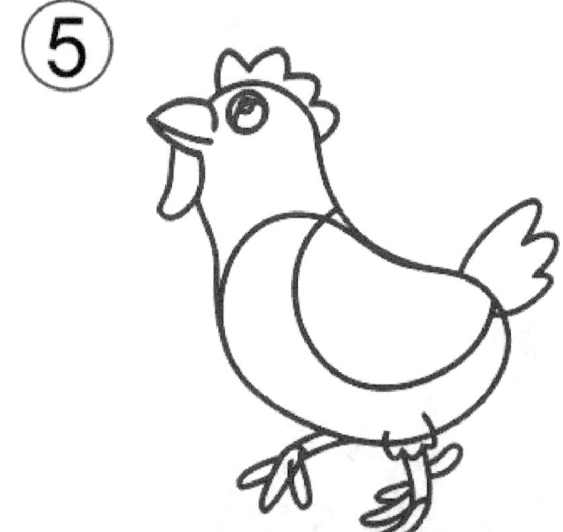

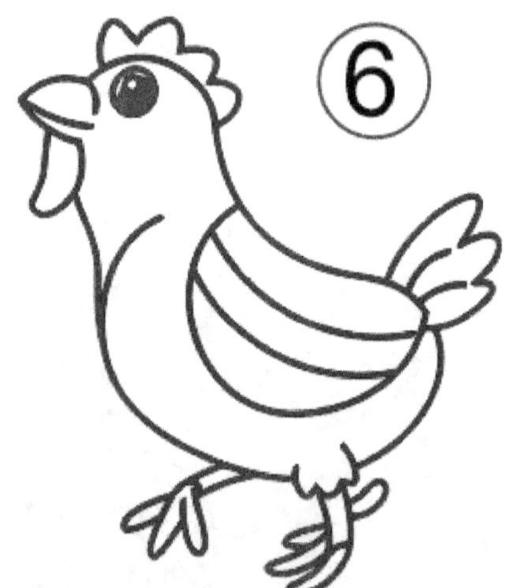

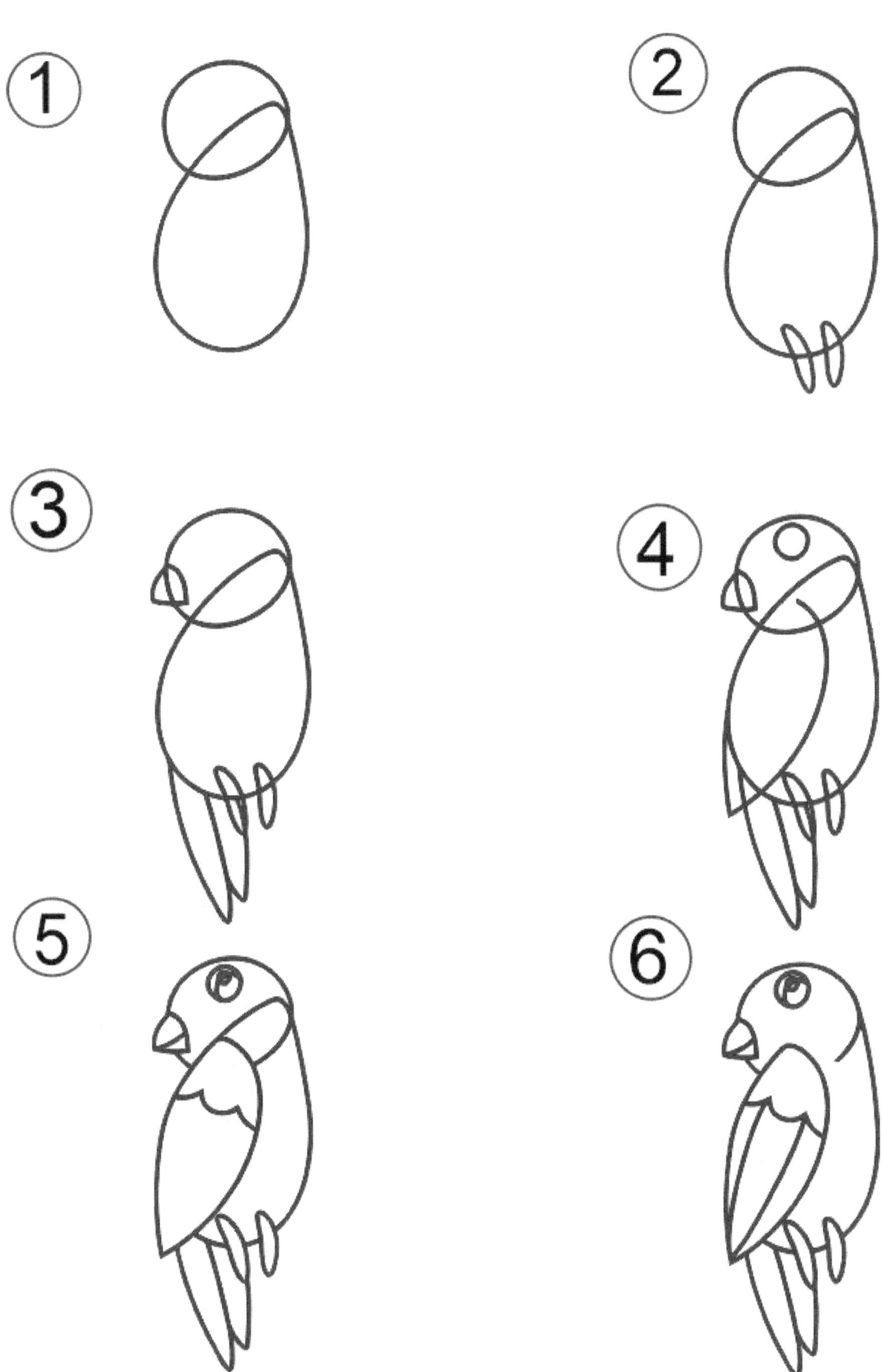

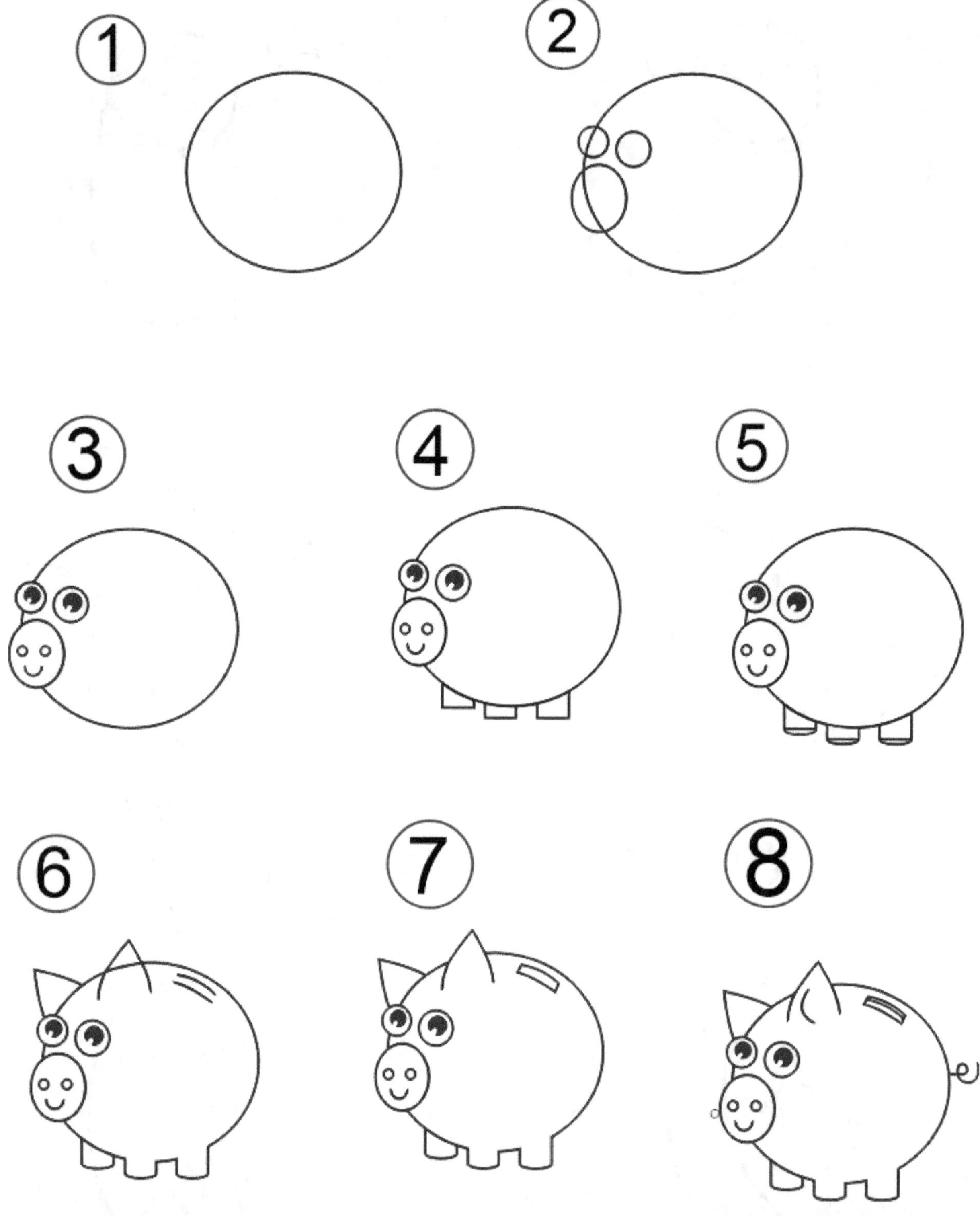

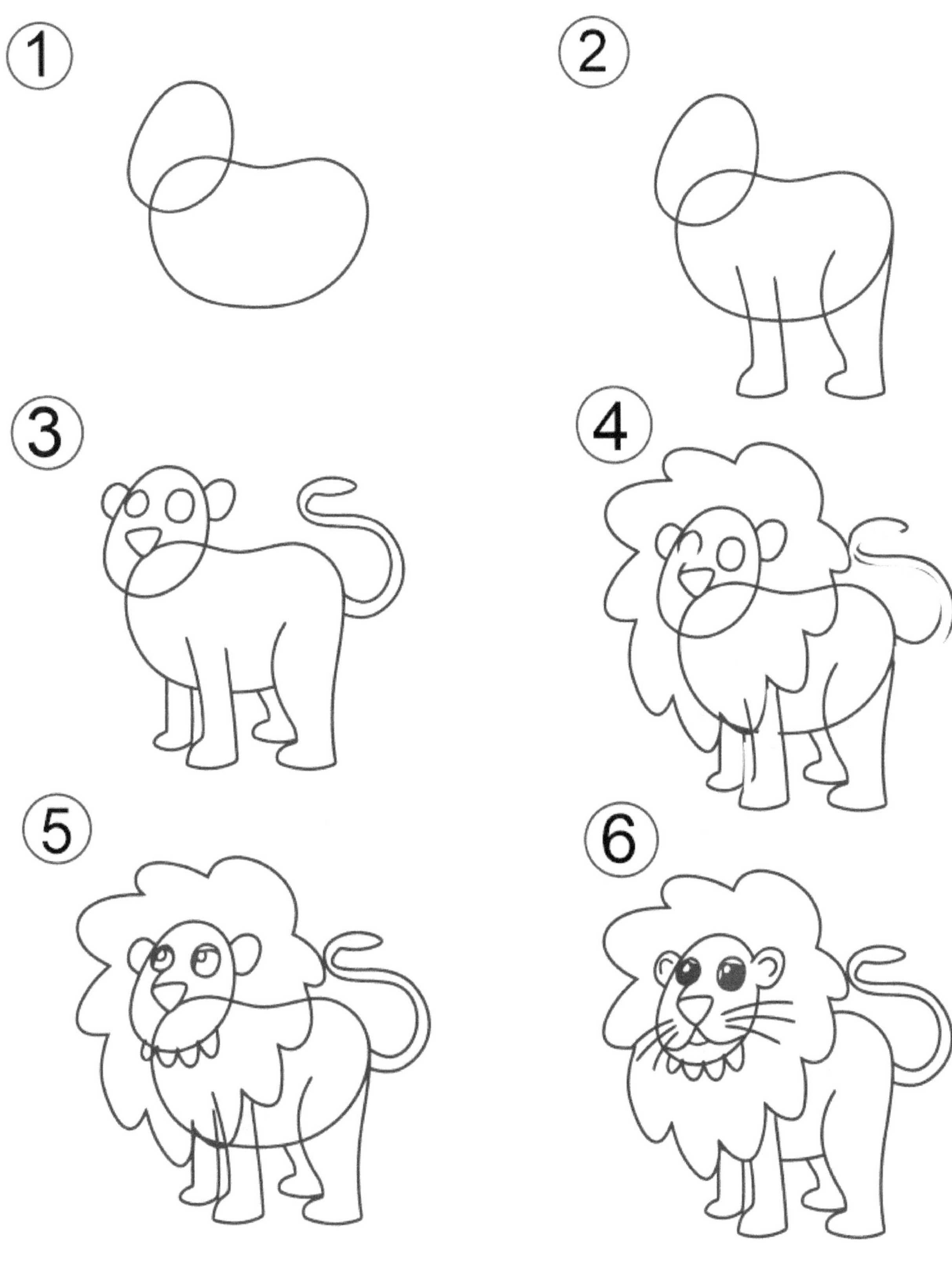

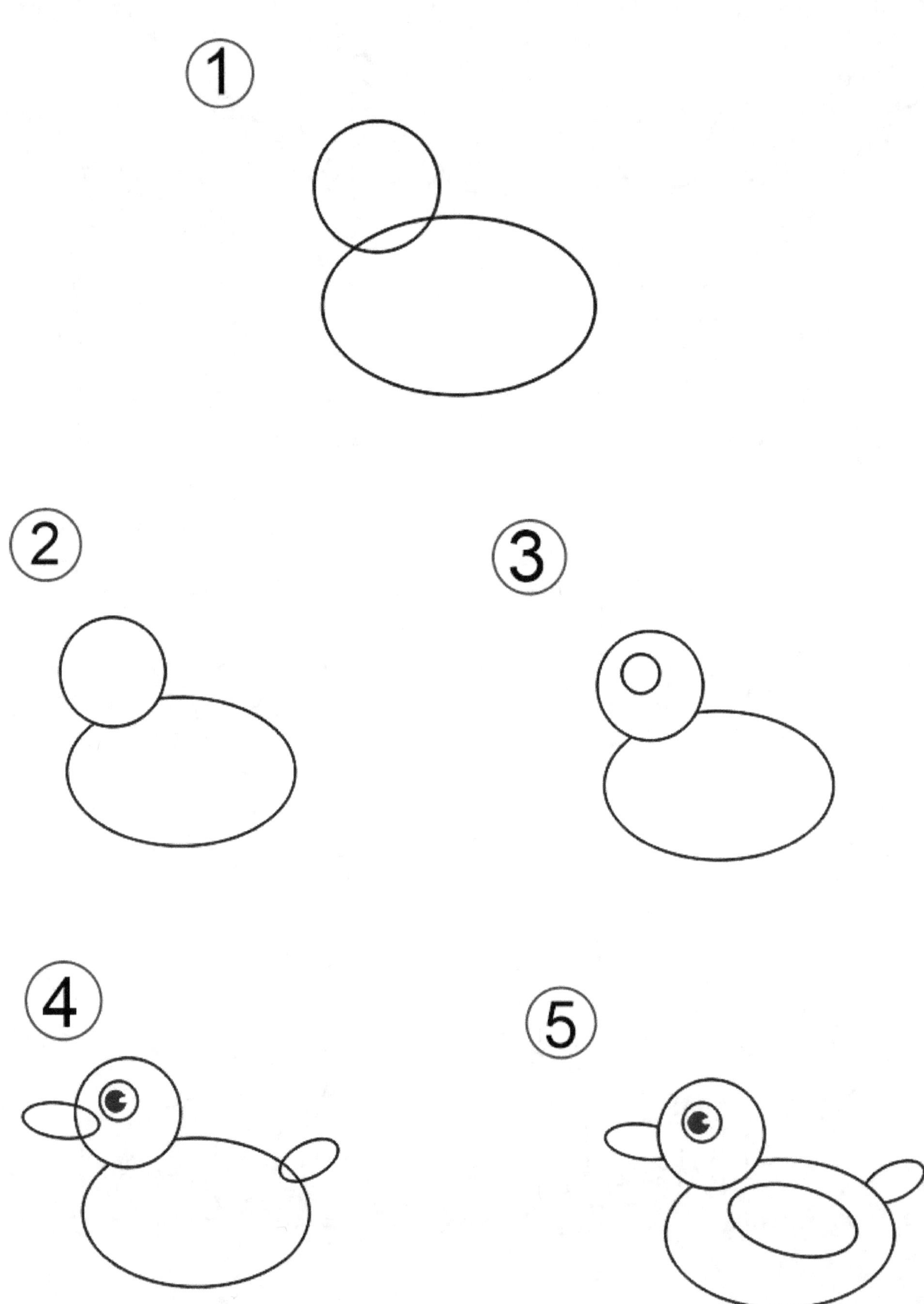
1
2
3
4
5

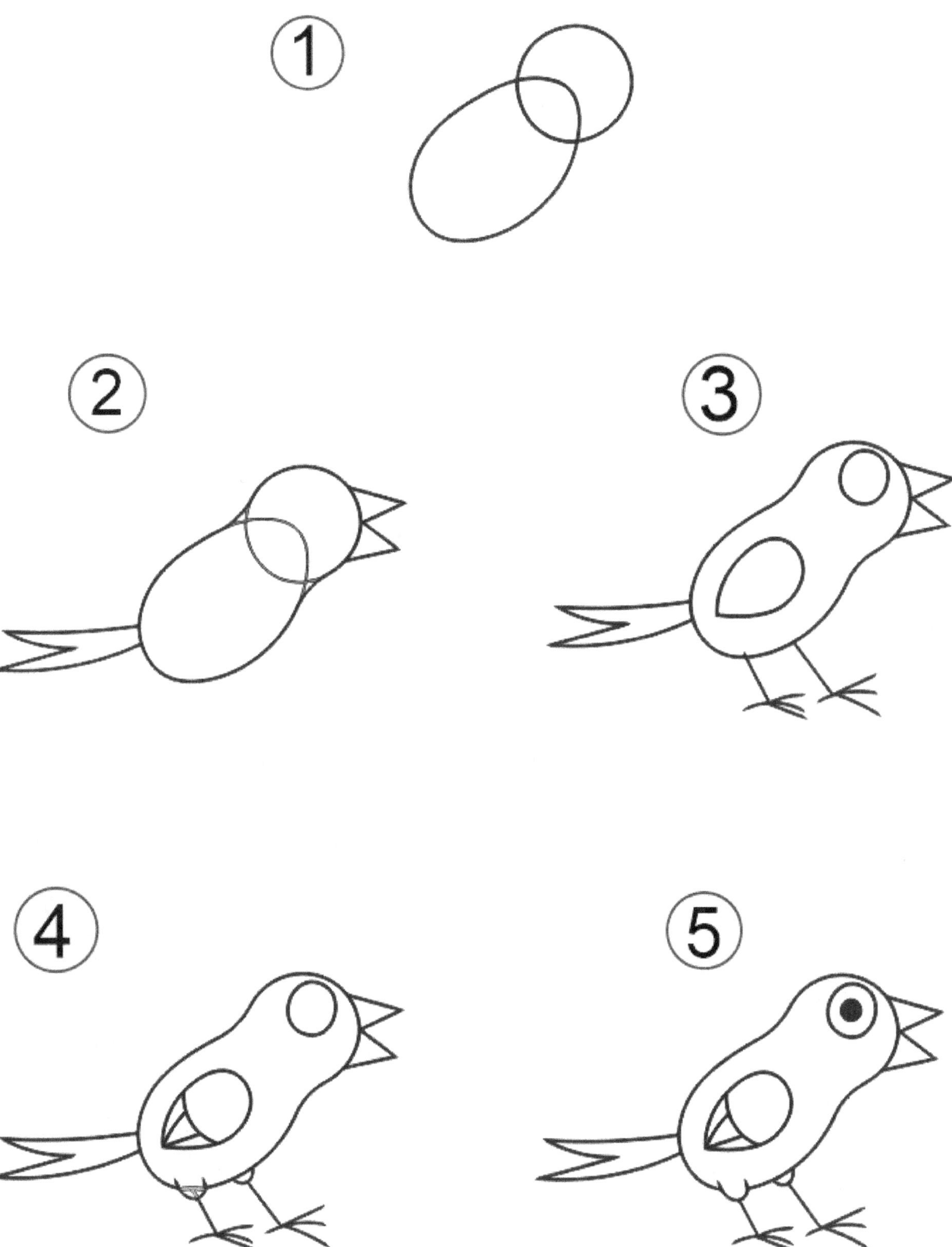

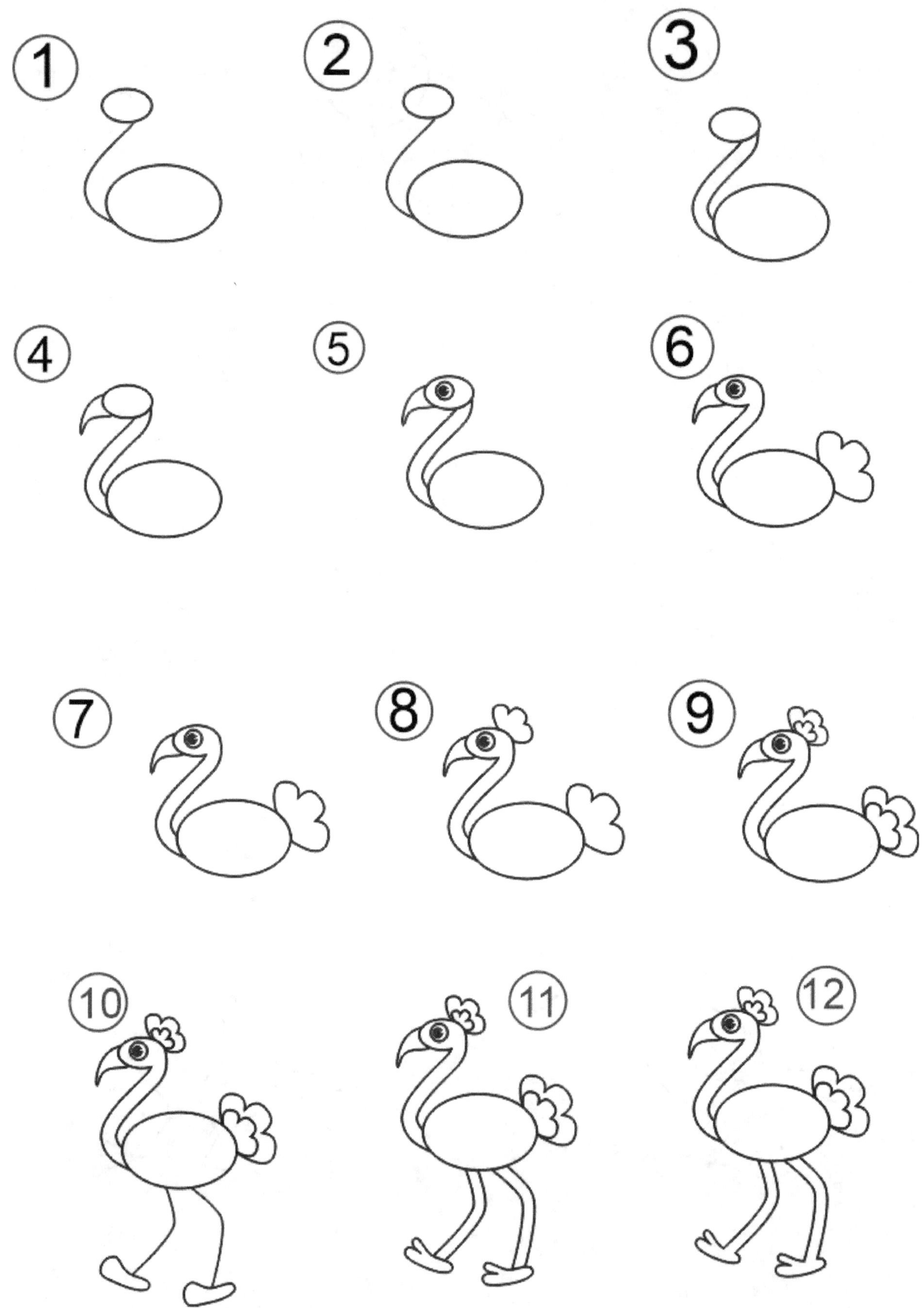

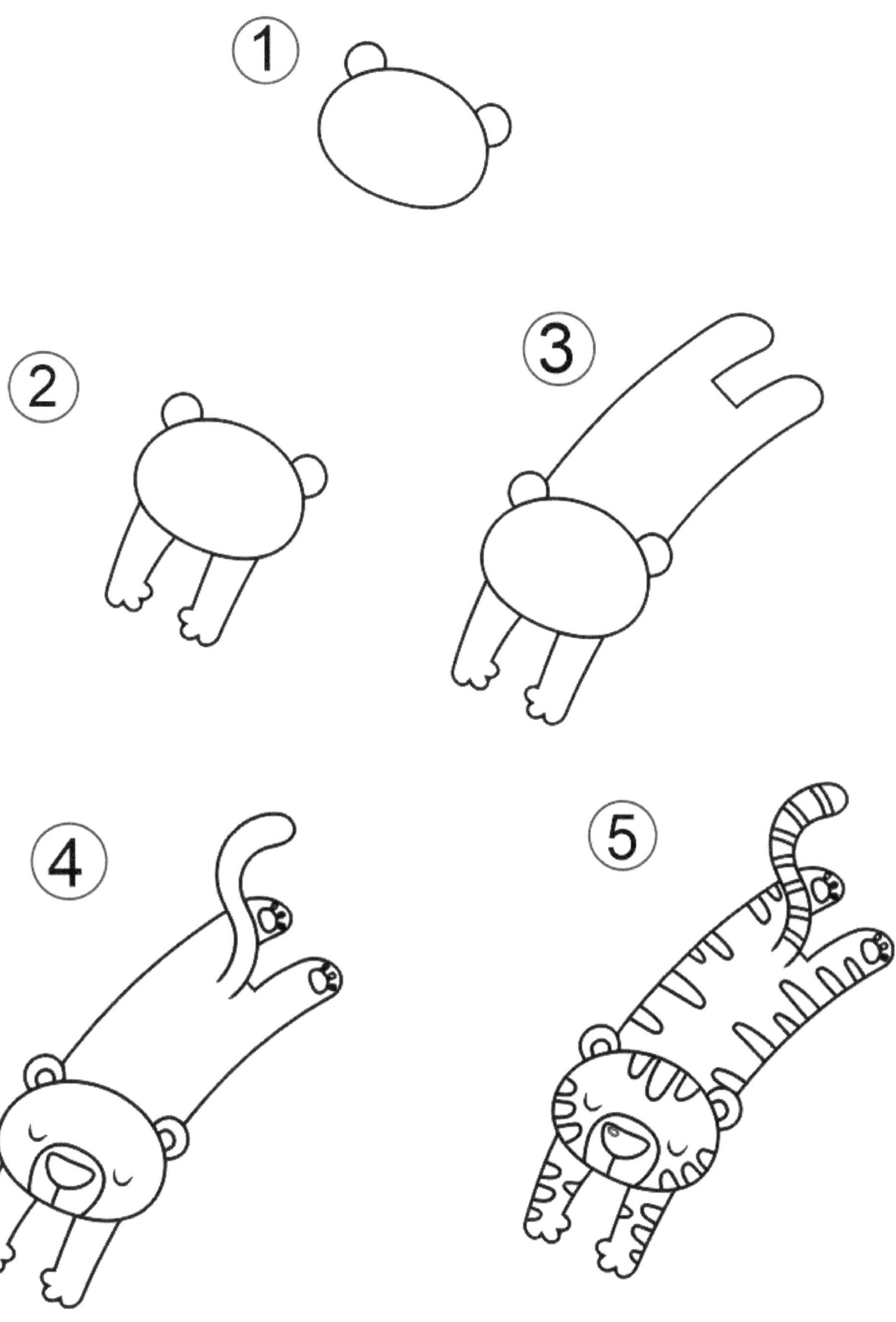

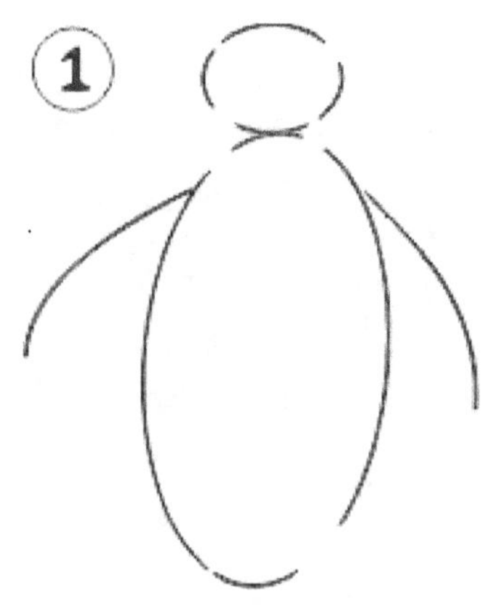

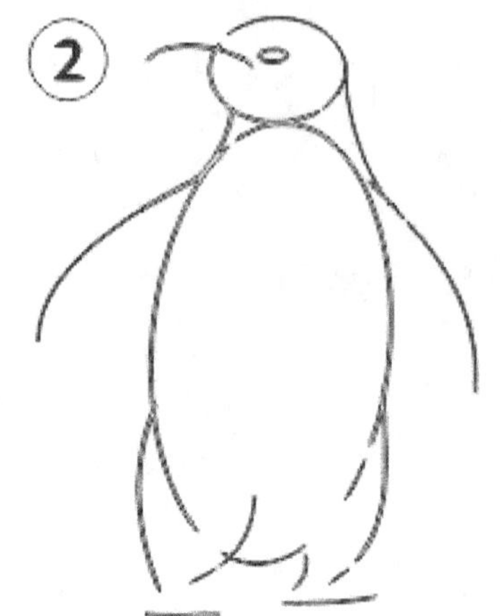

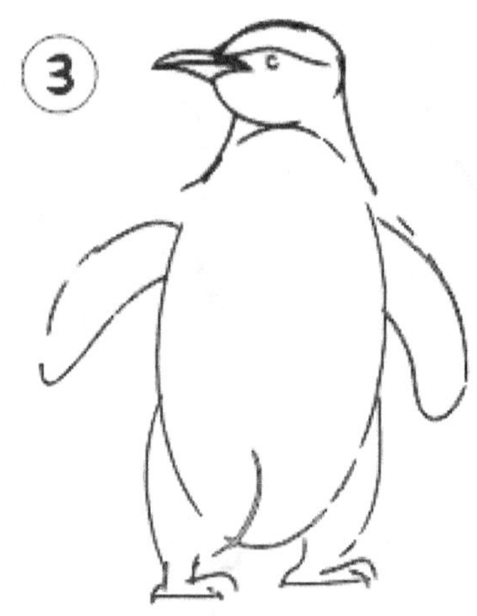

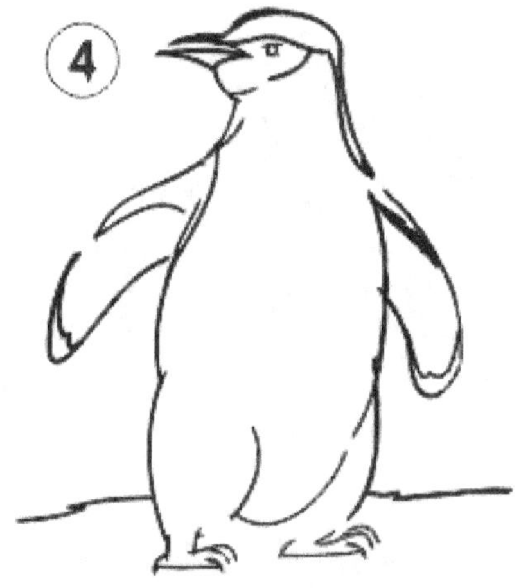

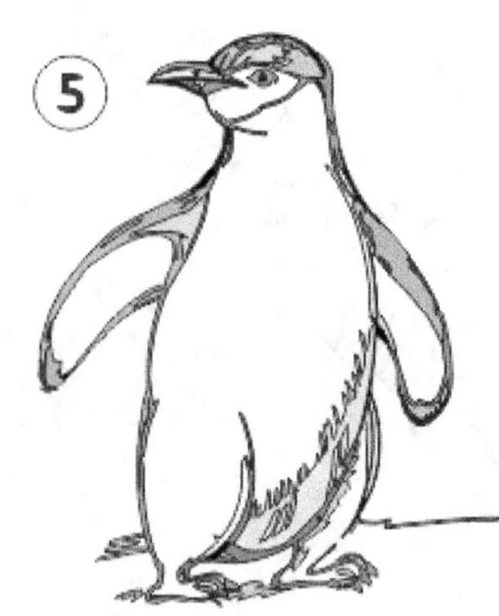

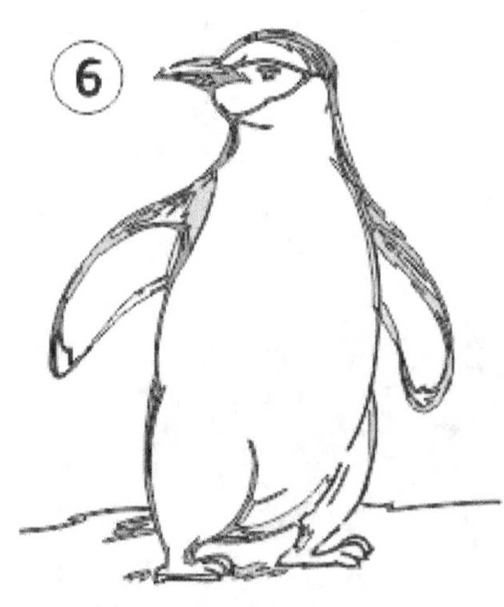

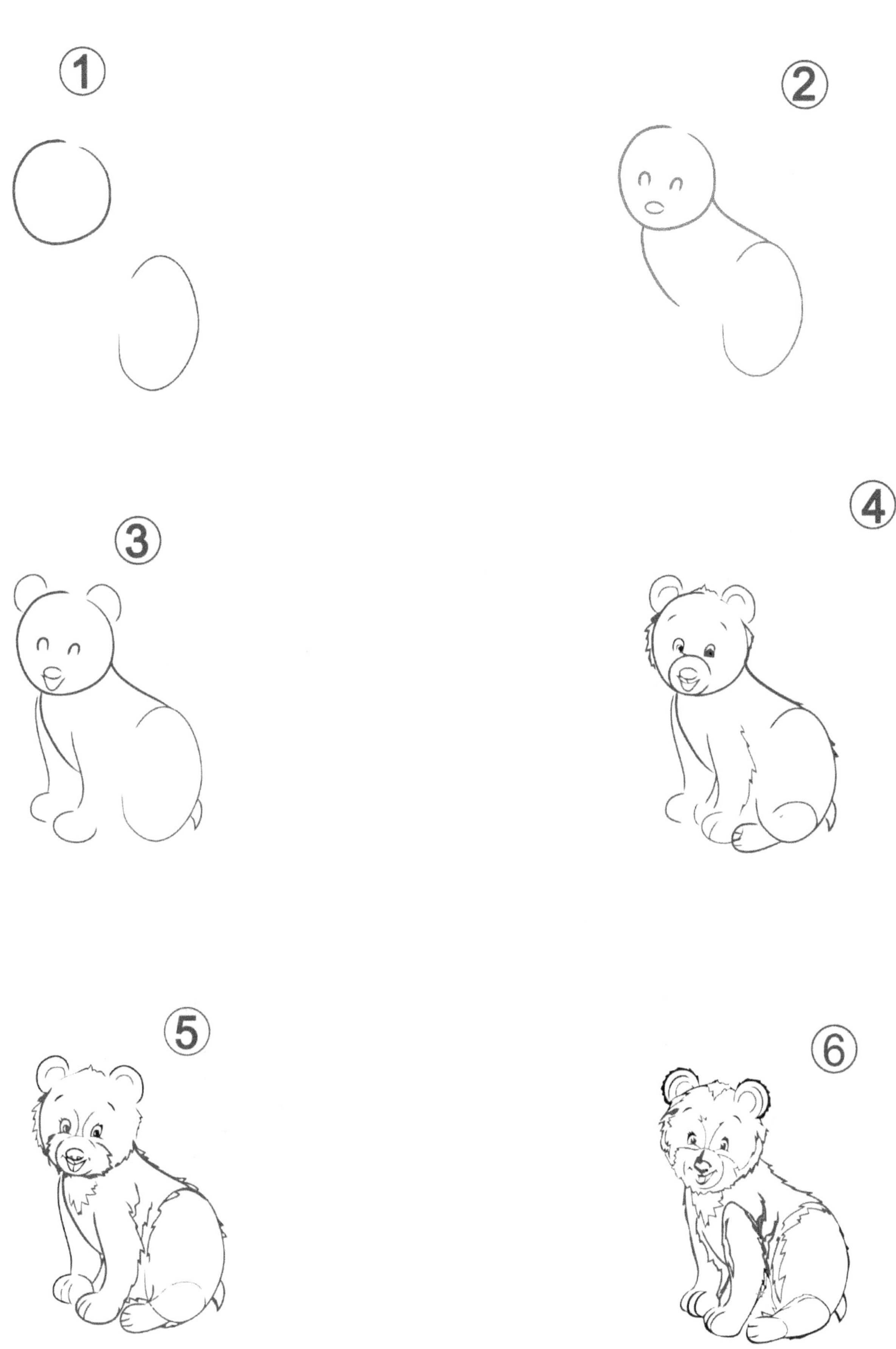

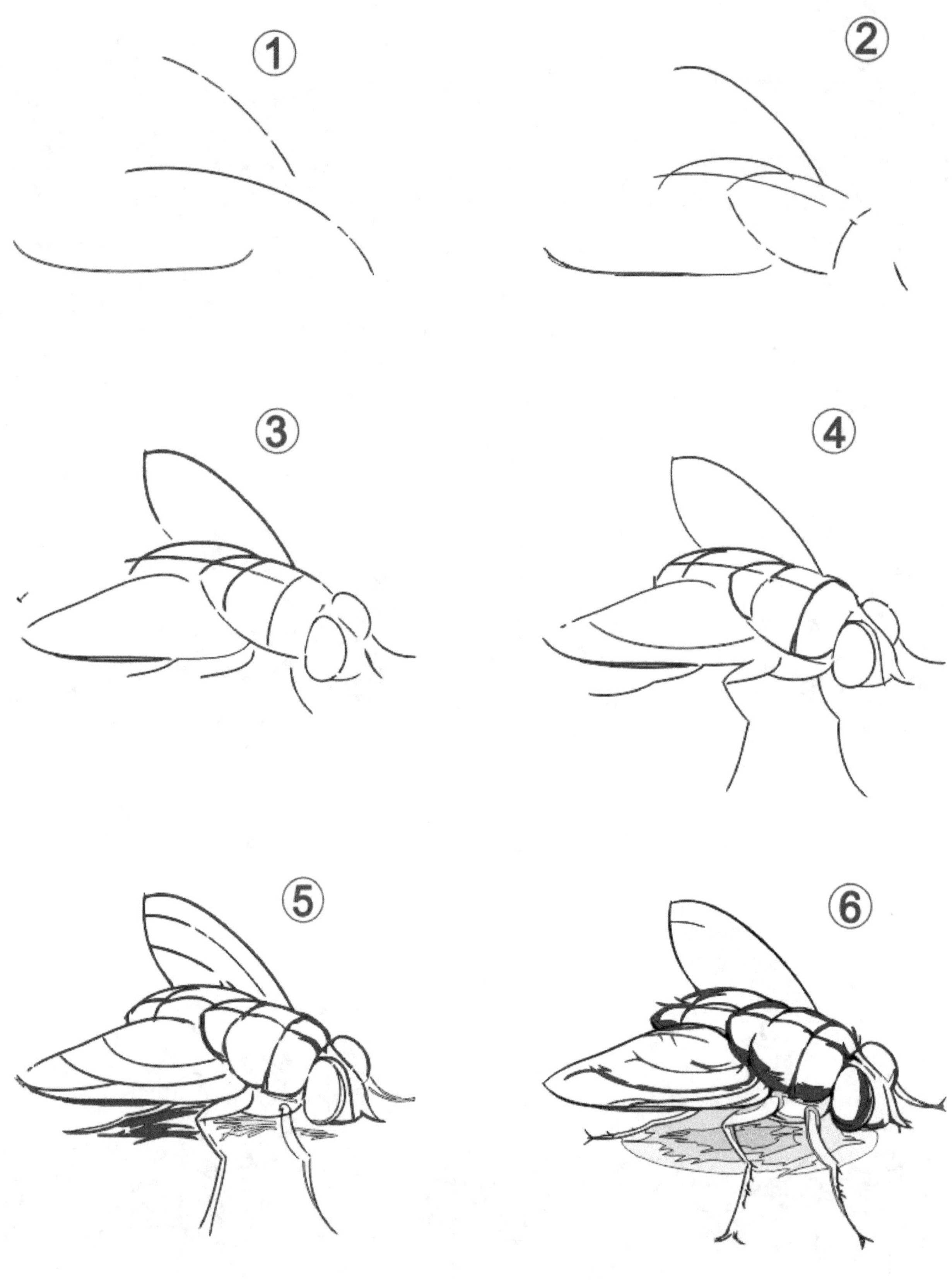

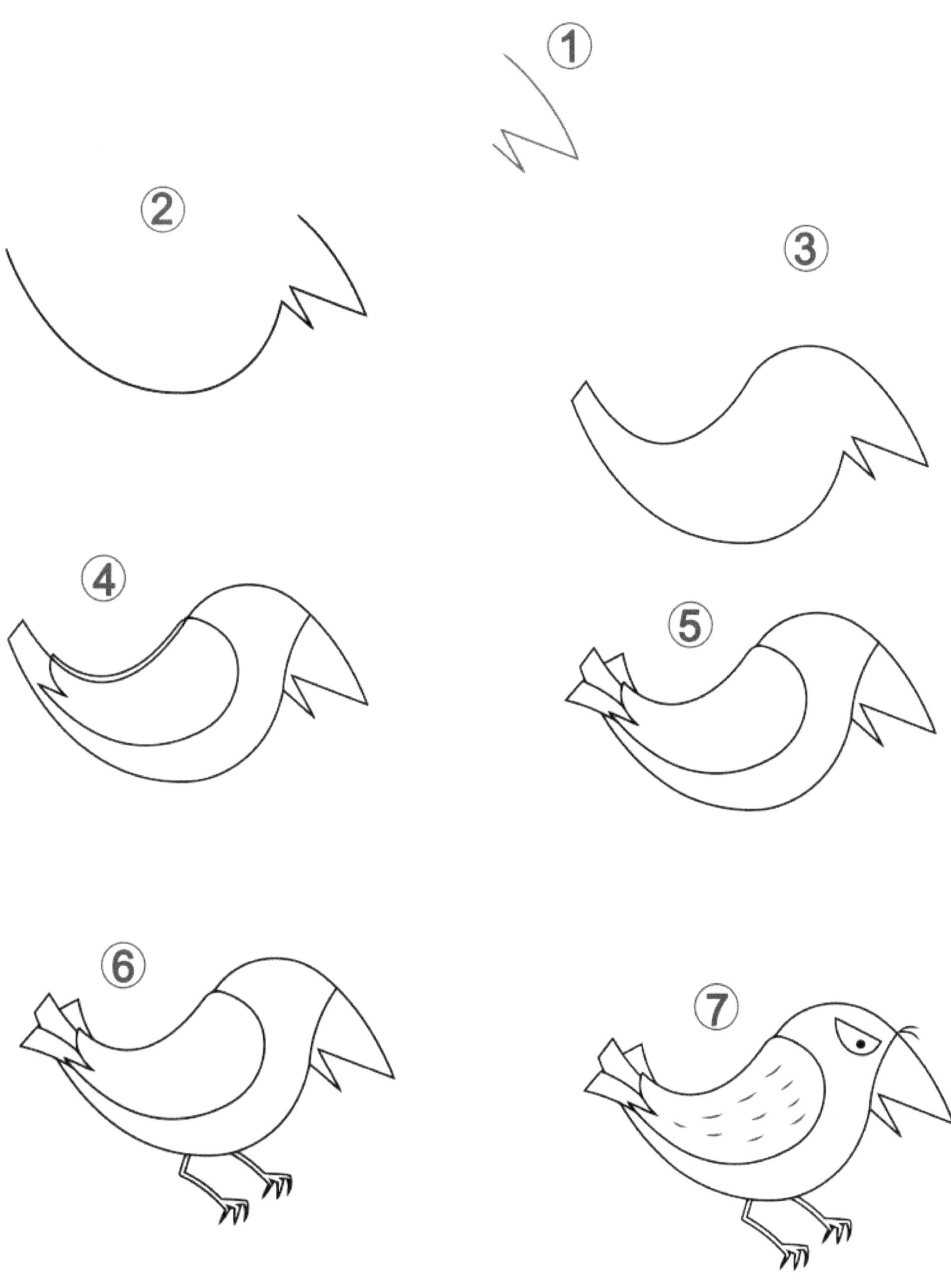

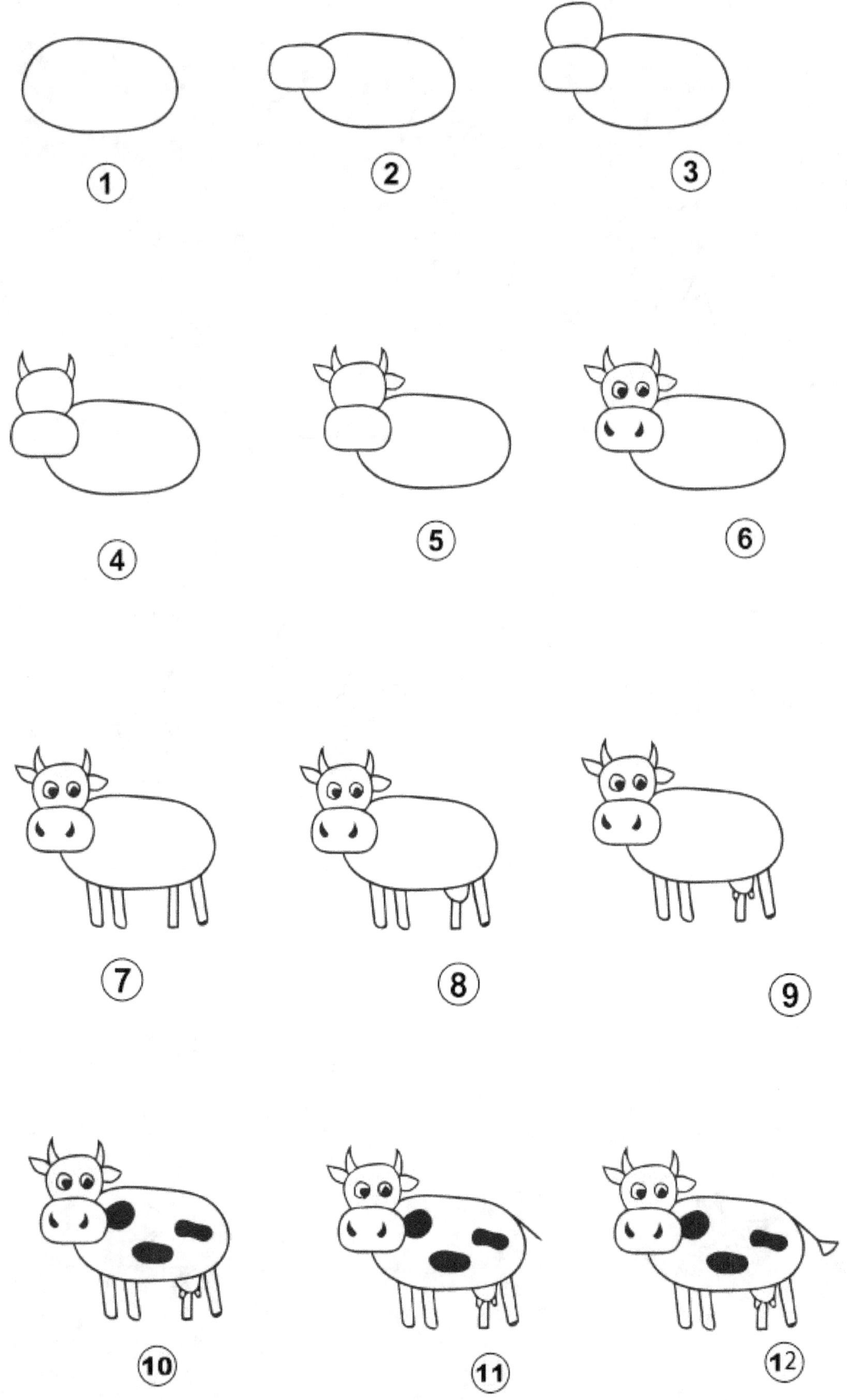

1
2
3
4
5
6
7
8
9
10
11
12

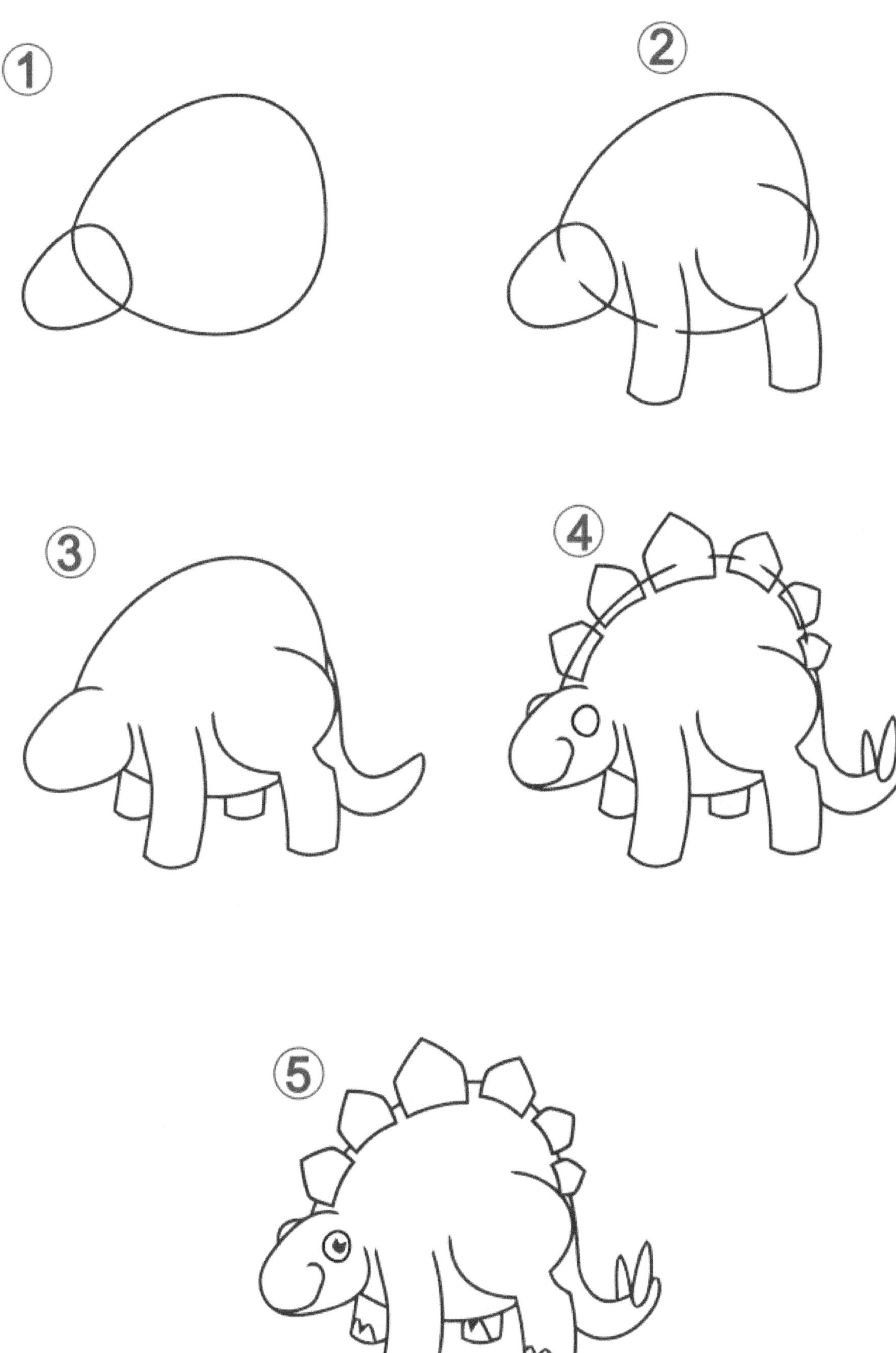

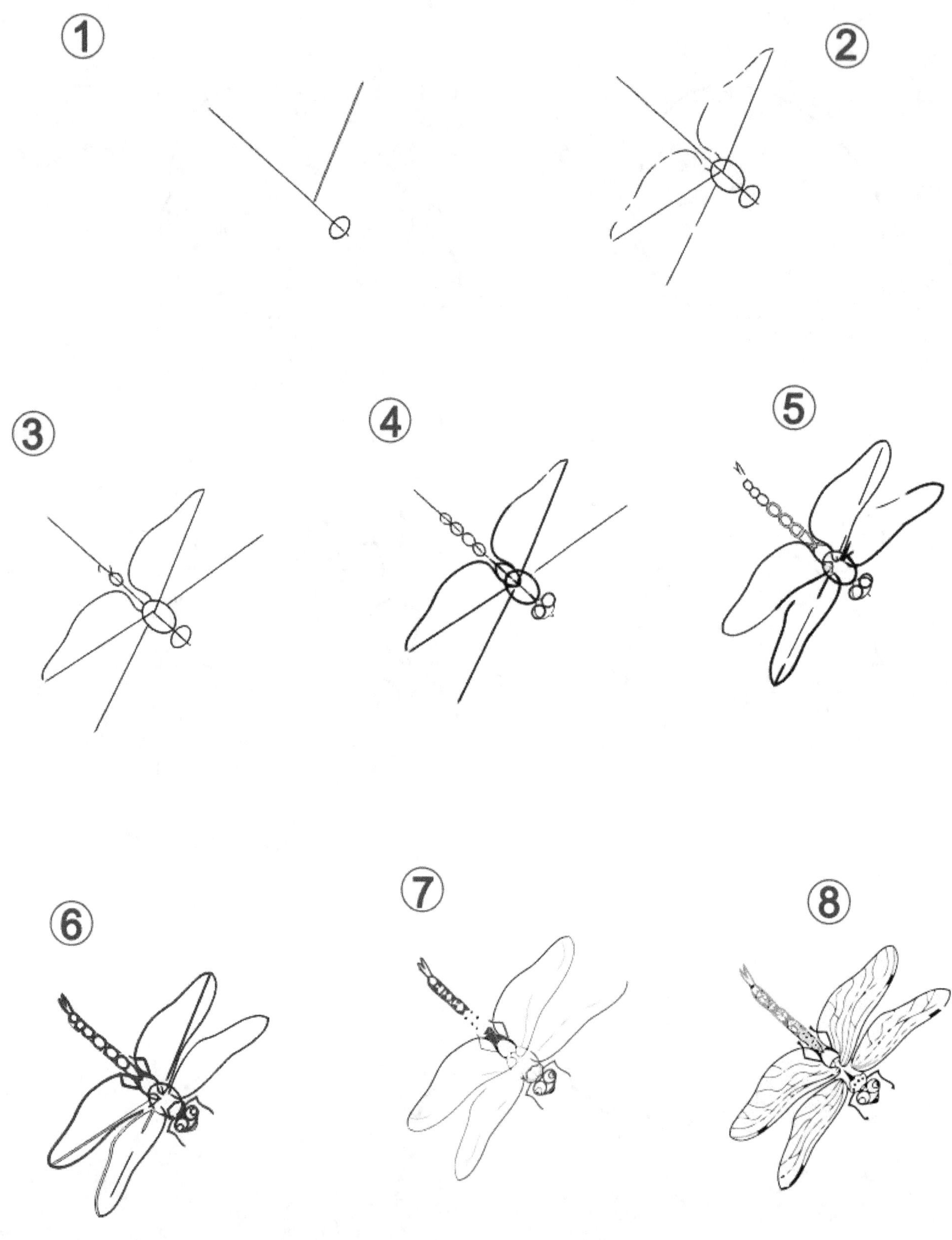

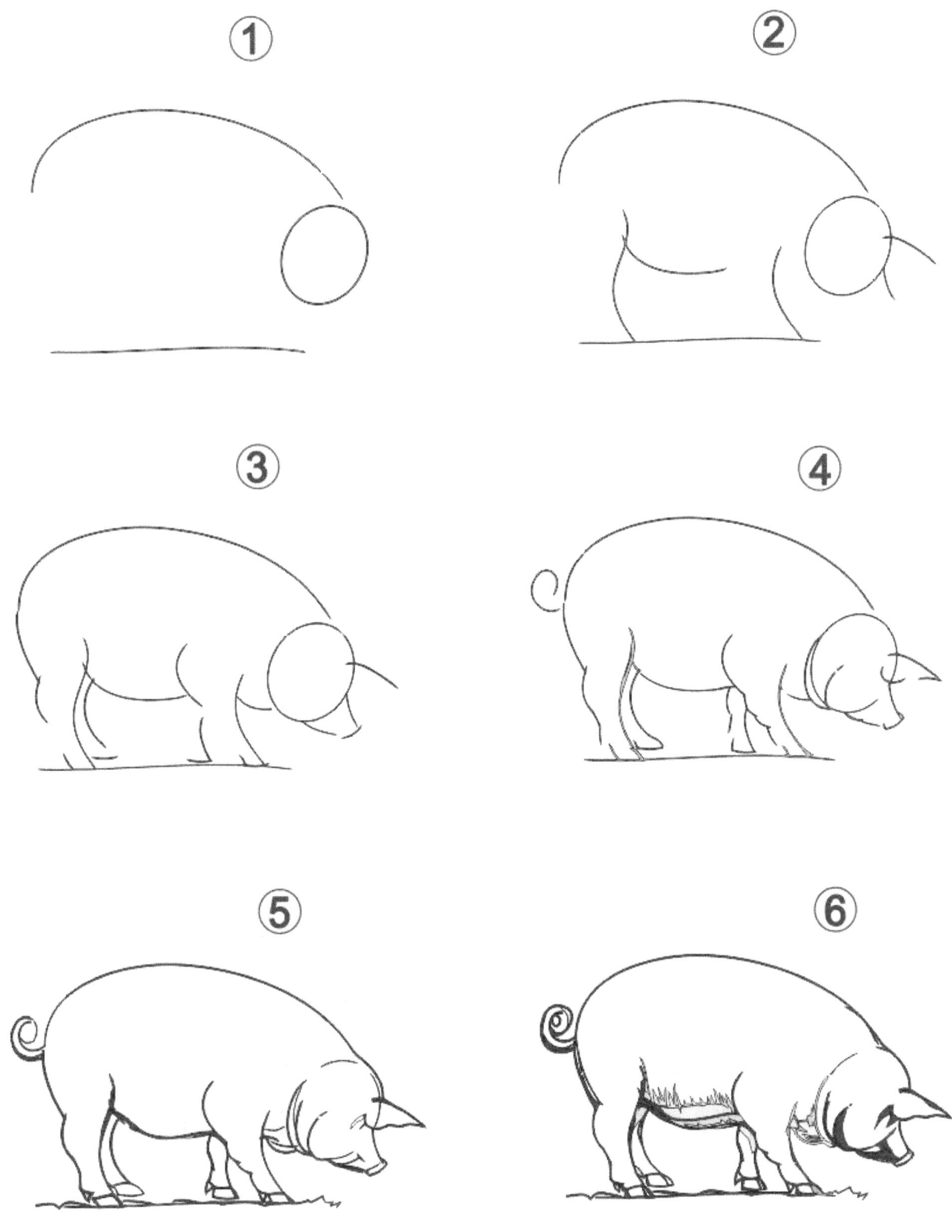

1
2
3
4
5
6

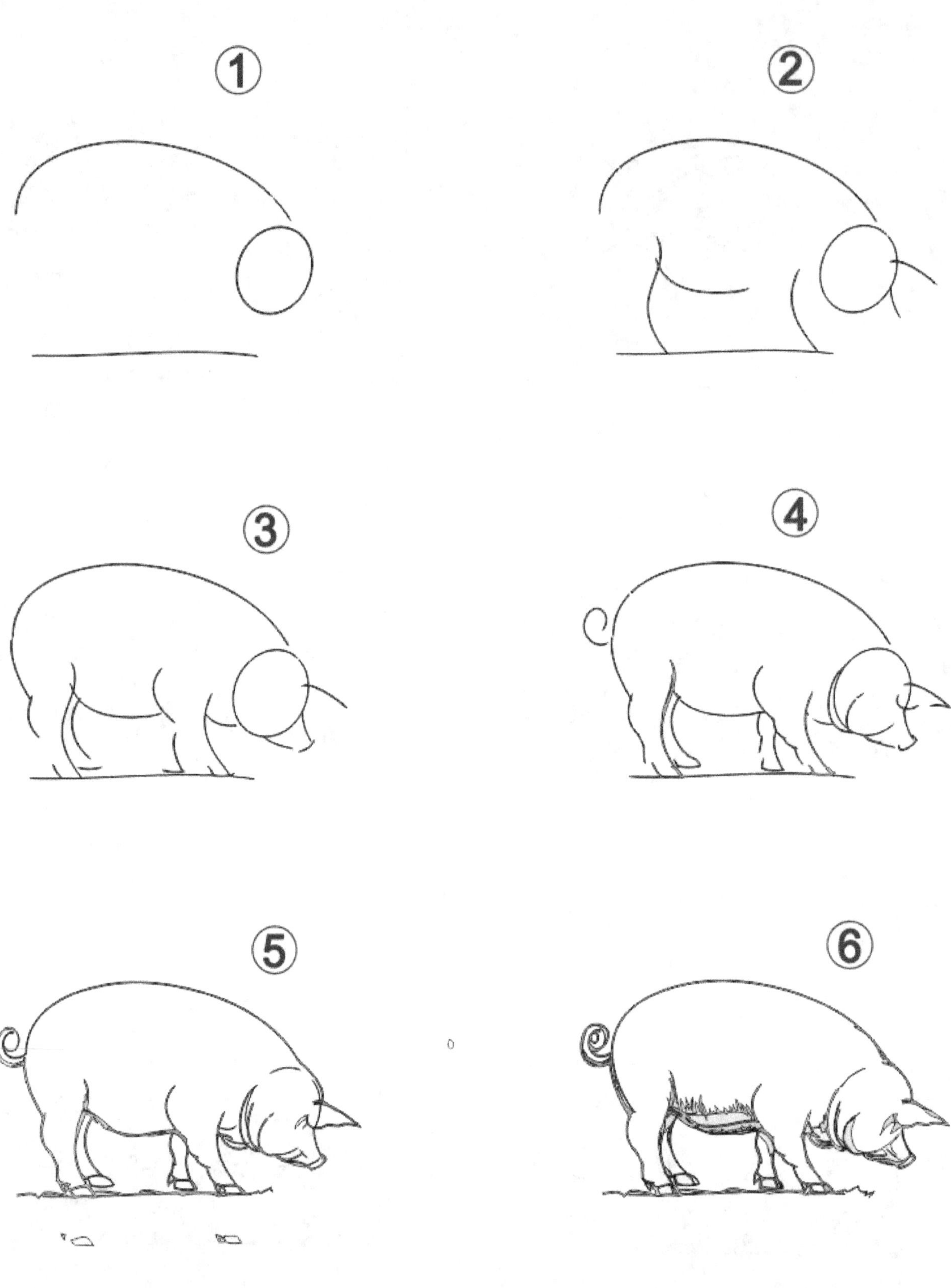

1
2
3
4
5
6